GREAT SIEGES

INTERNATIONAL LIBRARY

VEZIO MELEGARI

GREAT SIEGES

COLLINS London and Glasgow

© International Library 1970
© Rizzoli Editore, 1970

First Edition 1970
ISBN 0 00 100119 1

Printed in the Netherlands by Smeets Lithographers, Weert
Bound by Proost en Brandt n.v., Amsterdam

CONTENTS

Introduction

Throughout recorded history, from the days of the most primitive weapons up to the Second World War of 1939 to 1945, with its deadly and sophisticated methods of destruction, marching armies have been halted by strong points or other barriers, including fortified cities or regions.

At some time in a mobile war or a war of manoeuvre the armies were forced to halt and fight a positional battle, a static war. The greatest example of static warfare in all history is the First World War of 1914-18, when vast armies, living in trenches like troglodytes, faced each other for four years along a front of over 300 miles, with neither side able to break through the other's defensive barrier.

Fortifications, like weapons, were constantly being developed and improved. The walls of ancient cities that could keep a besieger at bay for weeks, months, or even years, would have stood little chance against the siege artillery of the First World War, but in their day they provided a strong and sometimes impregnable defence. Because of the strength of its walls any walled city could hold up an advancing army, so sieges have taken place in most of the wars of history.

As a result the development of weapons was a constant race between offensive and defensive. Against every new offensive weapon the defenders had to devise a new defence. And against new defences new offensive weapons had to be evolved. In ancient times men used bows and arrows and spears, but they needed more than such things to break down the walls of cities. Other methods were used against such defences–battering rams, pickaxes, techniques of undermining, and techniques of approach, including ramps, scaling ladders and mobile towers.

Battering rams and catapults were eventually replaced by cannon and these in turn by modern howitzers and guns firing high explosive shells. Many of the great battles of the First World War were siege operations; for example, the battle for the Belgian fortresses in the early days of the war and the assault on Verdun in 1916.

In this book the development of weapons from the earliest time to the most modern will be traced, and some of the famous sieges of history will be described in detail. The sieges described were in most cases decisive events in the wars of which they were part.

This relief on a metal roundel of a 15th century siege scene is in the Fine Arts Museum, Dijon.

CHAPTER 1

THE STONE
DEFENCES

There have been wars between groups, tribes and nations throughout the history of groups, tribes and nations and in almost all wars there have been sieges of longer or shorter duration. From the siege of Troy in ancient times to the siege of Leningrad in the Second World War, armies have been locked in combat for days, weeks, months—or even years. All sieges were attempts at destroying a main force of the enemy in some place that held up the attacker's advance and had itself great strategic or other importance.

The innocent suffer

In all sieges ordinary citizens, as well as armies, were involved unless the place attacked was a fortress and nothing more. But most of the great sieges involved towns or cities and the siege became total war. We often think of total war as being a modern phenomenon but in the siege context it is as old as history.

Women and old people killed at Avaricum by the Romans two thousand years ago were victims of war as were the citizens of Leningrad in 1942. Atrocities are part of the history of war. The Crusaders were stabbing children to death in the streets of Antioch 700 years before Hitler's SS. made extermination of Jews into a policy. Cromwell in his day destroyed the population of Drogheda and reported it without shame or regret.

Danger of siege

Likelihood or possibility of siege resulted in many cities having protective walls built round them and escape tunnels or ramparts for outer defences. The protecting wall of the city was therefore an armour of stone, and its origin lies in the distant past.

The beginnings of fortifications took place in pre-historic times. Palaeolithic man, living thirteen thousand years ago, fortified the entrance to his cave or built fires there as a barrier against sabre-toothed tiger and cave bear as well as against other human beings.

The idea of walls as a barrier grew as new methods of attack developed, with the result that man has been preoccupied with the idea of fortifications throughout his history. Let us look at the evolution of such fortifications.

The first fortifications

The earliest fortifications were attempts to improve the defensive qualities of natural barriers or features of the landscape, such as hillocks, slopes or crags, and can therefore be called field defences in the literal sense of the term. Field defences were built of earth, wood and stone and were the first true fortifications. The walls of ancient Italian and Greek cities are examples of such fortifications.

The first stage in the history of fortifications can be placed from the 8th

Sopkana Gate, Genoa. This gate was part of the wall erected in the 12th century for the defence of the city. At that time it was threatened by Frederick Barbarossa.

century B.C. to the 9th century A.D. During this long period fortifications were simply walls built, in the first place, of rocks piled on top of each other and later with stones specially cut and shaped to fit into each other in a more solid pattern. An example of the first, more primitive type of wall was built in 540 B.C. at Rome by Servius Tullius. The new walls round Rome erected by Lucius Aurelian in A.D. 271 are an example of the more advanced type of construction.

During a siege, the defenders took up their positions along the top of the walls. Some of the besieged dropped stones and other objects on the attacking troops. Archers shot their arrows from sheltered positions on the parapet. Every part of the wall was manned for counter-attack in such a way that the defenders were themselves protected to some degree from attack.

This 19th century drawing shows the cyclopean wall of the city of Ferentino. The wall is an example of the ancient megalithic type of construction,

The nuraghic complex at Barumini, most notable of Sardinian prehistoric defence systems which date back to the second millenium B.C. Nuraghes were built of blocks of stone set directly onto each other; no mortar was used.

The tunnellers

In some cases a covered tunnel ran along the inside of the wall. This gave protection to defenders moving about inside. The tunnels had small loopholes opening vertically, thought to have been invented by Archimedes during the siege of Syracuse, but in fact they were known before his time.

The walls at this time were like great garden walls, the top of the wall being level throughout its length.

Later the tower was developed. Towers were built at the corners of the walls on the perimeter, but they did not remain as a type of static defence. The tower structure was developed upwards and outwards in such a way as to form a flanking threat to an enemy outside.

A further development was the building of some solid type of fortification within the wall itself. The Greeks called this kind of fortification "acropolis", the Romans called it "arce". It was strongly designed as the last ditch defence of the garrison and to protect the town's valuables. This inner fortification was immediately sealed off at the beginning of hostilities.

Fortified frontiers

Until now the defensive wall had been designed to protect a town or a city or a single place. Inevitably, therefore, it covered a small area and was an enclosure. From this developed the idea of the wall as a regional defence or as a fortified frontier, a barrier covering a great stretch of country. A good example of this is Hadrian's Wall, built by the Romans to defend their English empire against attacks from Caledonia. Here the Romans built the highest ramparts, the deepest ditches and the strongest defences of their empire.

Hadrian's Wall, built between A.D. 122 and 126, was $73\frac{1}{2}$ miles long, 6 to 10 feet wide and 13 to 17 feet high. It had 300 towers and was protected by a moat 33 feet wide.

The fortified wall, despite its strength,

The defence walls of ancient Assyrian-Babylonian cities all carried the many-coloured ornamental motifs typical of that civilization and epoch.

was still exposed to direct assault. It could be approached by stone-throwing machines and it could be climbed by ladders or other assault machines. So the next stage in the development of fortifications was to protect the wall from close assault.

The answer was the ditch or moat. Dug in front of the walls and at some distance from them, it presented a barrier to the assaulting forces and compelled them to attack from further away.

Men and machines

At all times in history attacking troops have required some cover during their approach to a fortified position. In the ancient sieges many types of machines were used. The attackers themselves could form their own cover by using shields and one such formation was known as the "tortoise".

This "tortoise" was composed of a solid group of soldiers using their shields to cover the attack. The front line advanced with their shields held vertically in front of them while the following lines held their shields horizontally above their heads. Thus the unit was shielded in front and above.

But more efficient methods were evolved. One of these was the mobile wooden tunnel through which the army could approach. These tunnels were known as "vineae". Mobile platforms were also used and sometimes these carried a battering ram.

Siege engines of ancient times. Above, a tower devised for attacking walls. Below, a canopy known as a "tortoise" which protected the sappers at work.

The battering ram was an important assault weapon, not only in ancient times but also in the modern historical period. Originally it was literally a battering ram—a great beam of wood with an iron or bronze ram's head at its tip. Just as the ram uses its head for butting, the battering ram with the replica of the ram's head at its tip was designed to break down the enemy's wall. Strong walls needed great battering rams and great battering rams needed many soldiers to operate them. Writers men-

tion battering rams nearly 200 feet long, carried by hundreds of assaulting troops.

Assault by infantry

For direct assault by infantry, the old method was the use of ladder in one form or another; a method that persisted into the Second World War when rope ladders were used by the assaulting infantry of the Allies in the Normandy landings

to scale the cliffs from the beaches.

The old ladders had many forms. They were made of rope or wood. Some were simply ladders of the standard type, others had wheels at their base and hooks on top to grip the walls. The hook ladder was frequently used in the Second World War, a development being the use of rockets to carry the hooks to the top of a cliff or other obstacle. Even in ancient days, ladders were sometimes made of several pieces

and were thus the forerunners of the extension ladders in use today.

Julius Caesar

The Romans developed the assault tower and this was employed to perfection by Julius Caesar who was a master of fortifications and assault techniques. One of the Roman towers was 150 feet high. Its purpose was to carry infantry forward and launch them

The rock of Campidoglio in Rome under attack in 390 B.C. Legend has it that geese, bred and kept there for religious purposes, roused the defenders by their honking during a surprise attack by the Gauls.

Roman soldiers attack a besieged city by approaching the scaling ladders protected by a tortoise, in this case formed by their own shields held horizontally overhead. The defenders on the wall throw various kinds of missiles down onto the attackers.

Portrait of Vitruvius Pollio, Roman architect and writer. He was the author of a famous treatise in ten volumes, the last of which deals with the siege warfare and siege weapons of his time (1st century A.D.).

directly onto the top of the wall. They made their assault across a ramp laid down from the top of the tower.

Another assault machine consisted of a long beam, operated by a winch on the see-saw principle. When one end of the beam was lowered, the other came up carrying a cage or basket full of soldiers who leaped from it onto the top of the wall.

The Romans also developed the agger which was a ramp giving direct access to the wall. The agger was really a sloping road built under direct assault from the defenders. It was constructed of wood, earth and heaps of stones.

In defence of an empire

The greatest of all walls—it is still one of the wonders of the world—was the Great Wall of China. This great wall was built in sections which were eventually joined together into one great defence system by Shih Huang Ti who became first emperor of all China in the year 221 B.C. With other walls branching from it in certain places, the final length of the Great Wall was over 1,500 miles, its average height was more than 20 feet and it was up to 17 feet in width. Incorporated in its length were 25,000 towers.

The Great Wall was sufficient to stem the advance of small raiding parties, especially of cavalry, or parties without the means of demolition, but it would not have stopped, and did not prevent invasion by large well-equipped forces.

Fortifications in the middle ages

The second period in the history of fortifications is the Medieval Period, covering the 9th to 15th centuries. In this period defence works consisted mainly of small barriers or fences designed mainly for the defence of a single feudal unit or a small community. This was, of course, the era of the feudal system, introduced into England by William the Conqueror in 1066, and noted for its castles and turreted towns. Moats were excavated outside the walls of the castles.

Walls themselves were constantly strengthened and increased in number. Strong points were developed, the equivalent of the acropolis and the arce of ancient times. Fortified towers in the Norman period were known as keeps, and many of these still exist. Norman castles were virtually impregnable against assault.

The coming of the cannon changed all this and rendered obsolete all traditional weapons, such as spears and battering rams that had changed little since ancient times. Catapults were still used in the Middle Ages as were other engines of destruction like ballistas and traps, but these had no more power than ancient weapons.

The great Leonardo da Vinci designed many weapons of attack and defence but their value lay in their technical perfection; they were not new weapons.

With the discovery of gunpowder the

An episode during a medieval siege, from a sketch by R. Folcini. During his assault on the city walls of Crema in 1159, Emperor Frederick Barbarossa had eight hostages tied to one of the assault towers to be used in the attack. The citizens of Crema resisted the assault and during their counter-attack on the tower all the hostages were killed.

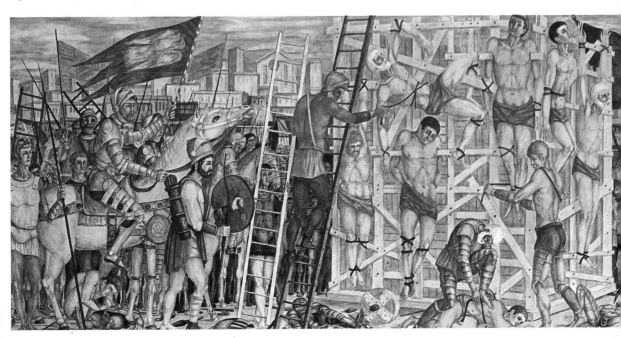

Two models of approach engines (a ladder and a covered tower) invented by Leonardo da Vinci. These models are in the Science and Technical Museum in Milan.

real boom period being from 1400 to 1500.

The period of ramparts

The modern age, in terms of fortresses and assault weapons, extends from about 1500 to the present day. The first of its periods was the era of ramparts which extended into the 19th century.

Ramparts were fortified buildings jutting out from the main walls and were a great aid to defence as any enemy advancing between them was automatically exposed to attack on the flank. Thus, if artillery blasted a gap in the main wall between ramparts the enemy could not take advantage of it without first dealing with the defenders manning the ramparts on either side. Breaching the wall was of little use if troops had to advance towards the breach while being attacked from both sides.

City ramparts became the order of the day and each European country had its specialists in this form of military design.

cannon rapidly developed. Artillery and fire-arms of all kinds improved and brought about a revolution in fortifications. Walls that had stood up to the battering of centuries were no defence against the new artillery, even at its most primitive. In 1450 Charles VII of France with his artillery drove the English troops from every castle in Normandy in the space of one year. This was in the period when artillery design was being rapidly improved, the

The siege of Aubenton, from a Flemish miniature of the 14th century. Note the mortar on the right, protected by a moveable shield.

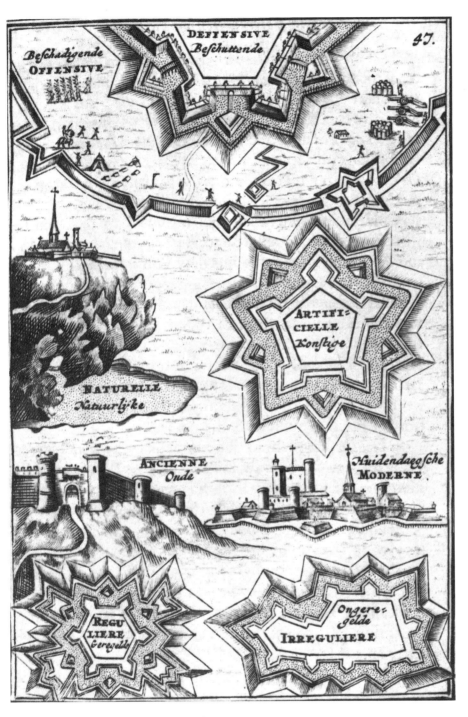

A 17th century illustration of various types of fortifications. They are here considered from the point of view of offence and defence. Below is an ancient double-barrelled cannon.

The modern period

The second part of the modern period was from 1850 to 1885 which can be defined as the period of entrenched fields and camps, of forts in walls and in the open field. Master of this style of fortification was the French general Montalembert who was responsible for the so-called "units of unattached forts". An outer ring of forts, separate from each other, held the enemy artillery attacks by counter battery fire while the fortified walls inside the ring halted

A battery at the 1849 siege of Vienna. Note the two huge fixed mortars.

Three examples of modern trench systems. The one on the left, of Paris, is dated 1844. Centre, Verdun with its encircling forts of concrete and steel. Right, the defence system at Metz with mobile batteries mounted on rails.

cavalry attacks. The distance between the ramparts and the forts was one or two miles. Forts on the Montalembert model were built at Koblenz, Cologne and Verona. And, of course, there was Paris, a walled city with 96 ramparts protected on the perimeter by 16 separate garrisons.

The third stage of the modern period stretches from 1885 to 1918. This was an era of field defences, of trenches, and of

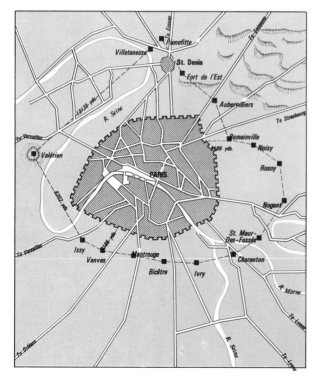

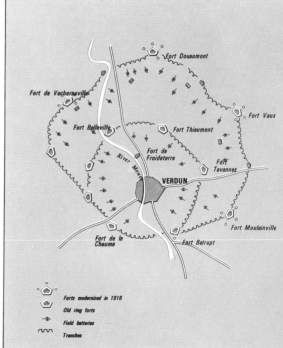

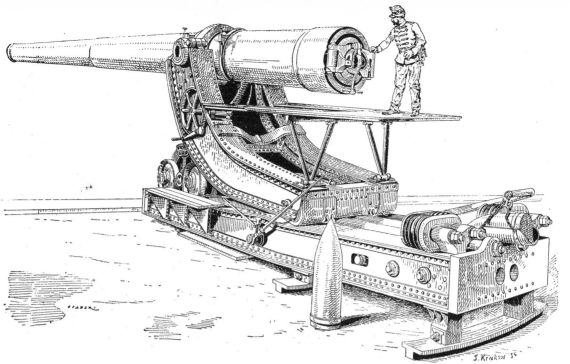

A siege artillery piece used by the French army at the end of the 19th century.

iron and concrete forts, but the increasing power of artillery made constant revision in the art of fortification necessary.

The French frontier

As artillery improved forts had become stronger, steel and reinforced concrete being increasingly used. General Brialmont was the father of the "armoured garrison" school in France. Forts built to Brialmont's specification substituted iron and cement for stone and beaten earth.

Another school devised the system of armoured forts. This school paid special attention to the gaps between forts and to areas where attacking infantry was likely to break through the defensive system. In such weak gaps or along such weak sectors strong points were built of cement and equipped with small calibre cannons and machine guns, either inside firing through slits or set in the open. This was the origin of what became known in the First World War as the "pill box".

The third school of the period was that responsible for the "separation of the defences". The basic idea of this school was to design buildings specially for close-up defence work and turn them into permanent fortresses, separate from the outer field works. The field defences were built wherever necessary and supplied with artillery to counter-attack early thrusts. These defences, therefore, were designed to delay or bog down assaulting infantry and to slow down the advance of field artillery while the main fortress remained intact.

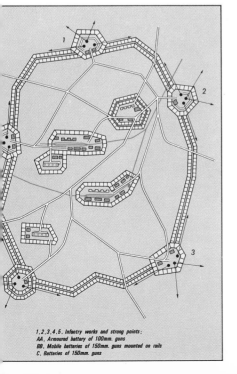

1,2,3,4,5. Infantry works and strong points;
AA. Armoured battery of 100mm. guns
BB. Mobile batteries of 150mm. guns mounted on rails
C. Batteries of 150mm. guns

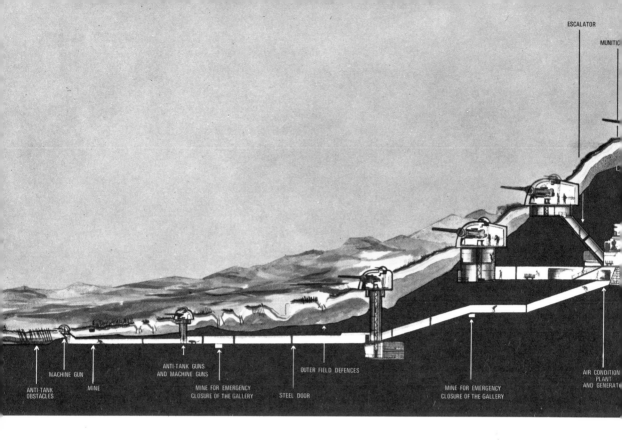

ESCALATOR

MUNITIC

MACHINE GUN

ANTI-TANK OBSTACLES

MINE

ANTI-TANK GUNS AND MACHINE GUNS

MINE FOR EMERGENCY CLOSURE OF THE GALLERY

STEEL DOOR

OUTER FIELD DEFENCES

MINE FOR EMERGENCY CLOSURE OF THE GALLERY

AIR CONDITION PLANT AND GENERAT

A vertical section of the French Maginot Line. This was the famous fortified line facing the Rhine that was to act as France's shield against German invasion. In the event the Germans went round the Maginot Line.

First World War

This system became the shield of France before the 1914-1918 War and great fortress systems were built around Verdun and Belfort. In Austria fortresses were built on the plateaux of Folgaria and Lavarone in 1914.

The great fortresses that met the shock of the German artillery in 1914 collapsed under the assault of siege guns of a size that no one had believed possible. The great howitzers that battered the forts of Liège had to be moved by rail and their like had never been seen before in war.

Yet later, during the Falkenheim assault on Verdun in 1916, the forts stood up to the blasting of millions of high-explosive shells, thus restoring man's faith in such fortifications. The great Fort Douaumont fell but it fell by default not by assault, and Verdun remained intact and an abscess in the German army's side.

Perhaps it was the great success at Verdun that created in the French army the Maginot mind that grew up with the

construction of the Maginot Line in the years between the two World Wars.

Fourthly and lastly, there was the school responsible for "perimeter strongholds of infantry". This envisaged the positioning of soldiers for close defence work while batteries of medium calibre provided more distant defence with the help of bigger guns mounted on railway gun-carriages and therefore highly mobile. This system operated at Metz. The railway gun was also developed as an assault weapon.

The Maginot Line

After 1918 developments and fortification became largely linear—the fortified line. First World War experience had persuaded commanders to replace the entrenched fields and armoured forts with the continuous fortress line.

The old forts had been sited close to the borders of the expected enemy and sited to bar all possible invasion routes, In place of this old system the French built their once famous and now discredited Maginot Line and in doing

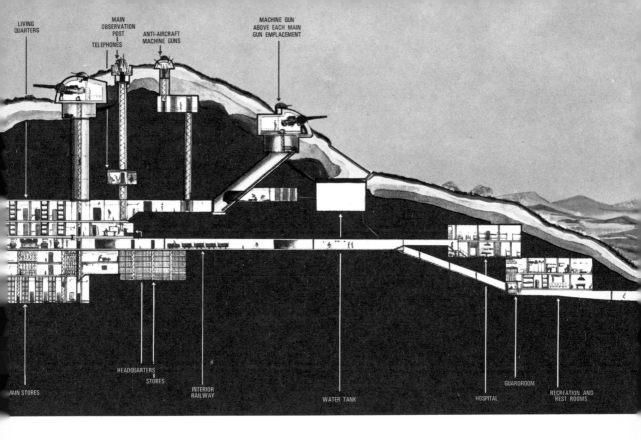

LIVING
QUARTERS

MAIN
OBSERVATION
POST
TELEPHONES

ANTI-AIRCRAFT
MACHINE GUNS

MACHINE GUN
ABOVE EACH MAIN
GUN EMPLACEMENT

HEADQUARTERS
STORES

MAIN STORES

INTERIOR
RAILWAY

WATER TANK

GUARDROOM

HOSPITAL

RECREATION AND
REST ROOMS

so created the illusion that they could sit behind the wall and let the war look after itself. The Germans on the opposite side of the Rhine built the famous Siegfried Line and Stalin followed suit in Russia with the Stalin Line.

The Maginot Line was never really tested. The Germans went round it via Belgium and Holland. The new fortresses in their path proved no obstacle.

There had been much talk of secret weapons that could destroy any fortress. In fact, the Germans used orthodox weapons and destroyed the forts by a highly organized combination of all arms—armoured units, artillery, mobile combat units and paratroops. They landed parachutists on top of forts to blow up the cupolas. The imaginative use of existing arms was the cause of destruction, not new weapons.

The Atlantic Wall

Finally, there was the Atlantic Wall which the Germans, in their propoganda insisted was impregnable. Sectors of this wall were highly fortified with concrete gun emplacements, pill boxes and other methods of defence, but in fact the Atlantic Wall was incomplete over much of its length and in some places it was a myth. The frontier the Germans had to defend was 2,200 miles long, running from the Pyrenees to Denmark, and it was impossible to fortify or defend it all at one time.

What of the future?

Atomic weapons and inter-continental ballistic missiles pose new problems of defence. Today there is in fact no defence. Strike and counterstrike would annihilate both attacker and defender. Traditional shelters and deep insulated trenches would be of little use in a modern nuclear attack and fallout shelters are still in their infancy.

Radar, pioneered by Watson Watt, proved its value in the Second World War and is still doing so. It can spot missiles as it could locate aircraft. But radar is not a defensive weapon itself although it may yet prove as important as it did in 1940-1945.

CHAPTER 2

THE SIEGE OF TROY

*"Was this the face that launched a thousand ships
And burnt the topless towers of Ilium?"*
MARLOWE.

Like poets before him and since his time, Marlowe, the English poet who lived before Shakespeare, chose the legendary Helen of Troy as one of his subjects. The two lines quoted refer firstly to the fact that the Greeks sent a great navy of more than 1,000 ships to the siege of Troy and the rescue of Helen. The second line refers to the burning of the tower of Troy which was also known as Ilium.

Paris and Helen

The story is that Helen, wife of the Greek King Menelaus, was abducted by Paris, son of King Priam of Troy, and the Trojan war was fought to rescue her. At least this is the story as told by the Greek epic poet, Homer, and even to this day the names of Helen and Paris go together like Romeo and Juliet, Dante and Beatrice or Tristan and Isolde. But how much of the story of Helen is true? And was her abduction in fact the cause of the Trojan war that led to the siege of Troy, perhaps the most famous siege in all history?

Troy stood on a hill, about one hundred feet above sea level, in Asia Minor near the point where the Aegean Sea narrows through the straits of the Dardanelles into the Sea of Marmora. The hill was called Hissarlik which, in Turkish, means "hill of strength". Troy, historically and according to Homer, was a fortress – that is, a walled city fortified against assault.

Homer's Iliad

The siege of Troy is the subject of Homer's *Iliad*, and it would be impossible to discuss Troy in any context without referring to Homer. There is no doubt that Homer's story has a firm basis in fact. He lived in the 9th century B.C., about 300 years after the siege which took place about the year 1184 B.C. His earliest biographers suggest that he was born in Asia Minor, so he would have been able to collect authentic details on the subject and record experiences of the siege that are still valuable from the historical point of view.

Apart from Homer the principal sources of present day knowledge about Troy are archaeology and mythology.

Archaeology and mythology

Archaeology is the science that studies antiquity from the remains of monuments, buildings and objects that were in everyday use in past ages. Unlike archaeology, history is based on the evidence of written documents or symbols in stone – for example, the Dead Sea Scrolls and Egyptian hieroglyphics.

The Poet Homer – from an etching after a painting by Raphael.

The Rape of Helen, which according to Homeric legend led to the Trojan wars, is shown in this painting of 1774 by Gavin Hamilton. In fact the Trojan war was the result of commercial and maritime rivalry.

The remains of the Scaean gate. According to Homer it was through this gate that the Greek Horse was dragged into the city. Near this gate Paris struck Achilles in the heel with his arrow. Below, a Trojan millstone and its pestle used to grind corn.

Mythology is the study of myths— a myth being a popular account of some great action that is a mixture of truth and fantasy. Myths grew from the spontaneous and free expression of human imagination and are not to be confused with the deliberate creations of Homer and other poets.

Specialized scholars, called mythologists, have collected and analyzed myths including those concerning Troy. The research of these people, together with the writings of ancient historians and Homer, will be the basis of this account of Troy, and its fiery and bloody destruction.

Heinrich Schliemann

The most important name in Trojan archaeology is undoubtedly that of Heinrich Schliemann. Schliemann was a German, born in 1822, who became a naturalized American in 1850 and died in Naples in 1890. He was not a professional archaeologist in the usual meaning of the word, but a gifted amateur following a boyhood dream with outstanding professional discipline and flair.

Even when he was at school he spoke of Troy and was laughed at for his addiction to Homer and the Greek heroes, and for his ambition to become

the discoverer of the ancient city. As a boy he was a great reader of books given to him by his father, who was a Protestant minister, and his interest in Troy increased with his reading.

He was a successful businessman who, before he reached the age of 50, could speak the principal European languages, ancient and modern. He became rich enough to be able to retire from business and devote the rest of his life to the search for the remains of Ilium. His wealth enabled him to pursue his dream and by his persistence he realized it – thus establishing the basic truth of the Homeric account.

Site of Troy

He went to Hissarlik, which had already been named by earlier scholars as the place where Troy must have been situated, and began his excavations on the wheat-covered slopes of the hill. Tradition had it that the city lay buried there. Schliemann found not one city, but nine, in successive layers. Which of them was the one he was looking for? Which was Homer's Ilium, the city destroyed by Agamemnon's Greeks?

Schliemann was convinced that Homer had lived at the time of the siege. He also reckoned that the time must have been the Iron Age because Homer mentions iron-cutting weapons and the Greek custom of cremating their dead.

But Schliemann's first discoveries were of another kind. He found statues, vases and jewellery of a non-Greek style, dateable at around 2000 B.C.— that is to say ten centuries before the Trojan War. This treasure he called Priam's treasure.

Too far down

What had happened was that Schliemann in his eagerness had dug so deeply into Hissarlik that he had by-passed the Ilium that he was looking for and discovered a more ancient and civilized Ilium than that of which Homer had sung.

Below this there was another prehistoric city and above it a further seven. It was later on that Schliemann discovered, in the seventh layer from the bottom, the Ilium of Homer, the Troy of Helen.

Here he discovered traces of fire. This beyond any doubt was the fire which, according to Homer, had ended the siege of Troy. Archaeologists and ancient historians were in agreement as to its period—about 1184 B.C. Whether it was a decade or so earlier or

A view of the excavation of Troy from a photograph by Heinrich Schliemann, the founder of modern archaeology. The photograph was taken during his excavations at Hissarlik in 1875.

Zeus, king and father of the gods, intervenes in the siege of Troy by hurling thunderbolts at the Greeks. Fresco by John Demin in the Papava Palace, Padua.

A composite picture of the Trojan war, from a 19th century drawing based on an ancient bas-relief. Note the outer walls at the top and centre and the Greek ships below.

later makes really very little difference.

Troy therefore had existed not in the Iron Age but in the late Bronze Age, at which time the Greeks had only pointed weapons and buried their dead instead of burning them. So Homer, on the evidence of his own poetry, could not have lived at the same time as his heroes.

Minoans and Mycenaeans

Greek civilization can be traced to two distinct peoples, the Minoans of Crete and the Mycenaeans of the mainland. The Minoan civilization of Crete, the mountainous Aegean island, flourished between 4000 and 1400 B.C. It was a wonderful civilization, called Minoan after Minos the legendary king of the island. Minoans were first-class seamen. Minoan ships and Minoan sailors had transported a mercenary army to Egypt at the request of the Egyptians whose country was at that time threatened by invasion.

These mercenary troops were the descendants of Balkan tribes that had occupied mainland Greece about 1900 B.C. and founded cities destined for everlasting fame—among them Thebes and Mycenae.

The entire Greek population of the period, together with its civilization,

were to take the Mycenaean name. The Greek civilization was therefore descended from the fusion of the gay, peace-loving Minoans and the warlike Mycenaeans.

Background to the Trojan war

According to Homer it was the Achaeans who attacked Troy ten years before the fatal year of 1184 B.C. The Achaeans were a part of the Mycenaean civilization – the second people to whom ancient Greece owed her greatness.

Quite suddenly, probably in 1500 B.C., something or some event totally destroyed the Minoan civilization of Crete. It could have been an earthquake; it could have been an invasion of Mycenaeans.

Whatever the cause the Mycenaeans went from strength to strength, becoming undisputed masters of the eastern Mediterranean and founding colonies at Rhodes and in Cyprus. In 1194 B.C. they launched their war against Troy, determined to destroy the city.

More than a city

Troy, on Hissarlik, was poised like a sentinel at the entrance to the Hellespont and therefore controlled the sources of copper, silver, iron, timber,

flax, hemp, dried fish, oil and above all cheap grain. It had contracted alliances with neighbouring cities, forming with them a confederation that posed a constant threat to Mycenaean commerce. It was this threat to which the Mycenaeans reacted.

According to Homer the pretext for the attack on Troy was the abduction by Paris of Helen, wife of the Spartan King Menelaus. This could have been true. There is no historical evidence either way, but any other reasons are not clear.

Meaning of "Helen"

"Helen" was the name of the Spartan goddess of the moon. The name Helen can also be taken as representing the great mother goddess who in the oldest Mediterranean religions was at the top of the divine hierarchy.

The story is further complicated by mythology which says that Helen was carried off first by Paris and then by the mythical hero Theseus.

Other mythologists claim that Helen, escaping with Paris while her husband was in Crete for his grandfather's funeral, took her son with her as well as most of the court treasure and three gold "talents" from the temple of the god Apollo. These mythologists

Another fresco by John Demin illustrates a critical point in the siege when Hector challenges Paris to continue the fight.

further claim that when Helen and Paris fled they were accompanied by five maids-in-waiting, including two ex-queens one of whom was Aethra, Theseus's mother.

Perhaps the only pointer towards the real truth in this whole story lies in the stolen treasure—with or without Helen. The Trojans, led by Paris, could have turned an official visit to the Spartan king into a piratical raid, in reprisal for something similar done to them by the Greeks. Put in blunter and non-poetical terms, the Trojan War could have been a settlement of accounts among pirates.

The War according to the Iliad

However, there was a war, and the siege of Troy ended it.

According to Homer, Helen's kidnapping outraged the whole of Greece and every city answered Menelaus's call to arms. They put soldiers and ships at the disposal of Agamemnon, king of Mycenae and brother of Menelaus.

A fleet of over a thousand ships sailed for Troy in the greatest military undertaking of this age of heroes and demi-gods. Their names were all to become immortal. Among the Greek host were Achilles, king of Thessaly and leader of the warrior Myrmidons, and Ulysses, king of Ithaca. Waiting for them in Troy were their heroic equals— the great Hector, son of Priam, and

Aeneas, the son of the goddess Venus.

Opening assault

According to the Homeric poem, the Greek army first attempted to take Troy by storm but they were repulsed with heavy losses. Agamemnon, the Greek commander, then decided to besiege the city.

The great fleet of ships was drawn up on dry land, which was the custom of the period, and ditches were dug to protect them from attack. Then the Greeks began to destroy neighbouring towns and villages and to raid deep into Trojan territory. But the Greek force was split when a quarrel broke out between Achilles and Agamemnon. This disagreement allowed the Trojans to attack and drive the Greeks back behind their trenches. Urged on by Hector the Trojans broke through and set fire to many Greek ships.

The legendary Achilles

Achilles took no part in this battle. He was still smarting after his quarrel with Agamemnon. His armour was being worn by his friend Patrocles, who challenged Hector and was left dead on the field.

Hector stripped the armour of Achilles from the body of Patrocles, This enraged Achilles, who donned

new armour and threw himself into the battle, thus rallying the wavering Greeks. Not even the great Hector could withstand him. Hector was killed and his corpse was dragged three times around the walls of Troy behind the chariot of the Greek warrior. Old King Priam begged Achilles on bended knee to return the mutilated body of his son.

Not long afterwards, Paris aimed an arrow at Achilles and mortally wounded him in the heel, the only vulnerable part of the hero's body. To this day, this part of the heel is known as the Achilles tendon. Thus a great warrior was lost to the Greek army. The arms of Achilles were claimed by Ajax but were awarded to Ulysses. Ajax sub-sequently went mad and killed himself.

The Wooden Horse

It now became a matter of urgency to break the siege and it was at this point that Ulysses conceived the idea of the wooden horse.

Under his direction a sculptor constructed an enormous wooden horse with a hollow interior. The idea was that picked warriors would be placed inside the horse and remain there in hiding. The other Greeks put to sea in their ships in the pretence of returning to their own country, and naturally the Trojans believed that their attackers had given up the struggle. They came

A passageway between the walls of the city of Troy, where soldiers gathered before sorties.

29

Troy dominated the
entry to the Hellespont.
This meant that it
controlled the trade
routes to the Orient.

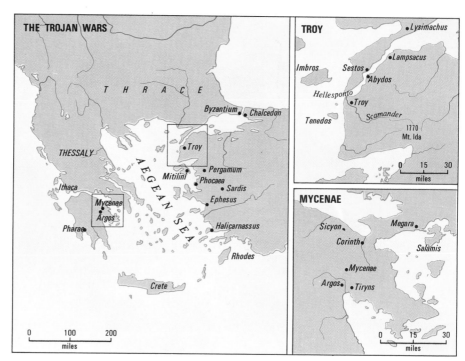

THE TROJAN WARS

THRACE

Byzantium • Chalcedon

THESSALY

AEGEAN SEA

• Troy

Mitilini
• Pergamum
Phocaea
• Sardis
• Ephesus

Ithaca

Mycenae
•
Argos •

Pharae

• Halicarnassus

Rhodes

Crete

0   100   200
        miles

TROY

• Lysimachus

Imbros   Sestos •
                        • Lampsacus
                      • Abydos
    Hellesponto
                    • Troy
    Tenedos   Scamander

                              1770
                              Mt. Ida

                        0   15   30
                            miles

MYCENAE

Sicyon •   Megara •
    Corinth •
                            Salamis
        • Mycenae
Argos • • Tiryns

                0   15   30
                    miles

out and took the horse inside the city walls, attributing to it some kind of religious significance.

This was exactly what Ulysses had planned. After dark he and his men climbed out of the belly of the wooden monster and signalled to the Greek fleet to return. The gates were thrown open and the Greek army poured in. In this way Troy was taken by surprise, its people slaughtered in their sleep and their homes pillaged and burned. A few managed to escape, among them Aeneas, who after a long journey was to settle in Italy with his people from whom the Romans are descended.

Such, briefly, is the story told in the twenty-four books of Homer's *Iliad*, although strictly speaking the *Iliad* deals only with the final year of the ten years' siege. Other sources reveal different aspects of the story, incidental perhaps, but necessary to any full account of the war.

The Siege

Trojan warriors, from
a reconstruction by
Ludovic Menin.

The Greek invasion was certainly preceded by raids along the coast of Thrace and Asia Minor. There was a Greek military outpost at the mouth of the River Scamander commanding the supply route from the Mediterranean to Troy. At the same time, it can be deduced from the *Iliad* that the siege did not completely cut off Troy.

Most of the time the inland routes were open although they were occasionally blocked when Achilles was on raiding expeditions. Trojan contingents, occupying Seatos and Abydis, secured the supply line to the city from Thrace.

The deciding factor was Agamemnon's decision to pursue a war of attrition until all the Trojan reserves had been used up. According to the *Iliad* even Hector admitted this. But the Greeks had some difficulty in keeping themselves supplied with provisions as the following story of Palamedes illustrates.

Discord in the Greek camp

Agamemnon had sent Ulysses to Thrace in search of grain but the Ithacan king had returned empty-handed. Palamedes

accused Ulysses of negligence and himself set off for Thrace, returning not long afterwards with a shipload of provisions. Ulysses's pride was hurt and he worked out a devilish plan whereby Palamedes was made to appear a traitor who had sold out to the Trojans.

As a result of this alleged perfidy, Palamedes was tried on the spot and condemned to death by stoning. It is said that before he died he uttered the famous words, "Truth you die before me."

Some historians and mythologists attribute the invention of dice and board games to Palamedes. It is claimed that these proved useful to the Greeks in passing the time during the long siege.

Palamedes has also been credited with the invention of lighthouses, scales, measurements, the discus and the alpha-bet. He can be looked upon as the epitome of Cretan culture and courtesy in contrast with Mycenaean uncouthness.

Homer and the Greeks

Homer is severe in his description of the Greeks. His sympathies clearly lay with the Trojan defenders who were, in any case, probably the descendants of other Greeks who migrated to Asia Minor some centuries earlier. They were the founders of the sixth Troy to emerge from Schliemann's excavations.

Troy itself, whether as revealed by the *Iliad* or by way of archaeological finds, was a fine city of "strongly built walls and broad streets". It was also known as the "city of wonderful horses", and it has been proved that these

The death of Achilles, from an 18th century painting by the artist Gavin Hamilton. Achilles was struck on the heel by an arrow shot by Paris and directed by Apollo. The funeral of the hero lasted eighteen days.

animals were brought into Asia Minor by the founders of Troy VI and Troy VII.

Modern research . . .

Troy VII, the Homeric one, seems to have been an overcrowded city with many "shanty town" areas, indicating that it had become necessary to find accommodation for a sudden increase in population. These houses might have been built for Trojan allies or refugees from the country, fleeing before the Greek armies. In Troy VI, great urns have been found that were used for storing food. In Troy VII the same urns were buried to the brims to save all possible space.

All over Troy VII were traces of fire and pillaging. Stretches of its magnificent walls still stand. These walls had strong towers over 50 feet broad and probably 30 feet high, with openings cunningly angled to expose the besieger to long-range attack by the defenders.

Against these walls the weapons of that time were largely ineffective. For offensive purposes long wooden spears, swords and daggers, bows and arrows were used. For defensive purposes bronze helmets and cow hide shields

The walls of Troy. Their ruin has not diminished their magnificence and impressive beauty.

were used. The cow hide shields were octagonally shaped, perhaps for some religious reason.

. . . and theories

In the siege warfare of the time, the attack had to be made either with ladders or through cracks in the wall. Troy fell perhaps because the use of a mobile wooden tower bristling with armed men and covered with dampened horse hides, against which the flaming torches and burning pitch thrown down by the defenders was of no avail.

The point at which this wooden and hide tower was used to assault the wall could have been in the west wing where, according to the *Iliad*, the battlements were weakest. At this point, near a fig tree, the Greeks, led by Agamemnon, tried three times to storm the city.

The Trojan Horse

The story of the wooden horse comes in rather late. The earliest commentators, like Homer, are inclined to believe that it was really a kind of battle machine. Others argue that it was a horse painted on a side entrance to the city which was opened to the Greeks by a Trojan

traitor, Antenor. Yet others consider that a cavalry attack brought about the fall of Troy or maintain that the Greeks, to distinguish themselves from the enemy in the dark and confusion of battle, wore a horse emblem.

There is a picture of the Trojan horse in the Florence Museum of Archaeology cut into a stone which once adorned a ring. The horse is on the oval, and on the back are two ladders leaning against the walls of a city. There are men climbing up the ladders, so evidently the artist was following a different interpretation from Homer's.

A possible explanation of the Trojan horse lies in comparing the Florence drawing with two similar depictions, one of which comes from Pakistan. It is a relief drawing of a woman with arms raised, standing on top of a wall. Perhaps she is the great mother of the Mediterranean, symbolizing the Trojan legend of Helen.

The warriors are approaching her as if she were symbolic of long-hoped-for victory, just as in the most distant past young boys reached maturity after a ceremony in which they were shut up for a time in a construction resembling an animal. Symbolically swallowed by the animal they acquired its strength and were considered grown men.

In Greek mythology the horse symbolizes the passage to the Beyond, and could also stand as the symbol of the Greek victory over Troy.

A reconstruction of the gigantic horse of Troy, used in a television production of Homer's Odyssey. *According to legend a group of warriors, guided by Ulysses, hid in its body.*

CHAPTER 3

AVARICUM AND
ALESIA

At the time of Julius Caesar, Gaul was divided into three main regions—Aquitania, and the lands of the Belgae and the Gauls or Celts.

In the words of Caesar; "*Gallia est omnis divisa in partes tres*". This sentence must have been photographed on every schoolboy's memory like Caesar's three point alliterative announcement, "*Veni vidi vici*" (I came, I saw, I conquered).

No schoolboy learning Latin could escape being drafted into Caesar's Gallic War because the great Caesar left a most detailed account of his campaign. His books are required reading for anyone studying the history of the period.

Although he lived more than two thousand years ago, Julius Caesar is probably better known as a military commander than most of the generals of modern history.

Caesar's commentaries

He was born about 100 B.C. and died in 44 B.C. He spent the years 58 to 50 B.C. subjecting Gaul, a part of the world that corresponds roughly to present-day France. Then it was peopled by barbaric tribes that, at the time of Caesar's campaign, were in revolt against Rome.

Caesar did not write of these campaigns simply as accounts of battles. Having overthrown the Republic and raised himself to a position of great power he had in some way to explain his actions to his contemporaries and to posterity. He wrote what he had to say in his books of *Commentaries on the Gallic War*.

The Gallic War, *De Bello Gallico*, was written in 52-51 B.C. which was when the sieges of Avaricum and Alesia took place. There was, therefore, no need for Caesar to tax his memory recalling events. He was writing mostly while they were fresh in his mind. In any case, he had at his disposal records of the campaign in addition to his own notes and the despatches that he had sent to the Roman Senate.

What is known of the campaign comes directly from the commentaries of Caesar himself, but before we examine them we might look at the methods of siege warfare of ancient, and especially Roman times.

As we have already seen in the case of the siege of Troy, an attacker had to fall back on the method of blockade if he failed to take his objective by direct assault.

In blockading a city the Romans constructed round it a double belt of fortifications, one facing the besieged city and the other in the opposite direction towards open country. This was a great undertaking which required large numbers of men. The inner ring or belt of fortifications protected the besiegers against attacks or sorties by the besieged. The second belt protected them against attack by allies of the besieged who might be try-

This monument to Vercingetorix, designed by Aimé Millet in 1865, was erected on the site of Alesia by order of Napoleon III.

35

ing to break through from the outside.

The inner belt was usually sited about one hundred yards from the city walls, which put it out of range of any missiles that could be thrown from inside. Traps, ditches and various other obstacles were placed in front of the inner ring as a further protection and to make it almost impossible for the besieged citizens to make a sudden rush on the position. Attacks of this kind were always to be expected, especially in the first and final stages of a siege, as we shall see in the case of Alesia.

Methods of attack

Once the inner and outer fortification rings had been completed the besiegers had three different ways in which they could attack their objective.

The first method was to move great wooden towers, mounted on wheels, against the walls. The towers were either protected by shields or by a fixed or mobile platform like a roof.

Using their towers the attackers then tried to break down the walls with battering rams or pickaxes. Battering rams were great beams of wood with armour-plated heads.

The besieged garrison defended themselves by throwing stones to break through the roof of the tower. They also threw down torches to set the

shields on fire. To counteract this the attackers would put sodden mattresses made of fresh skins on top of the shields.

The defenders in turn let down quilted curtains against the walls to soften the shock of the battering rams. They also lowered large hooks with which they tried to catch and pull up the battering rams.

Although it would appear that the defenders in such a situation were in the stronger position, the attacker had many advantages. This was so well recognized that Vitruvius Pollio, a contemporary of Caesar and author of a most important architectural work, strongly advised the citizens of a besieged city to pile up earth in front of the walls as the only sufficient means of defence.

The second method used by a besieging army was the underground attack, which was carried out along a tunnel with a mine at the end of it.

Mining–old style

The word mine in this context must not be confused with modern explosive devices. The invention of gunpowder lay many centuries in the future. But the Romans and Greeks knew and practised methods that achieved results

in much the same way. The attackers drove tunnels right up to, and underneath, the city walls. As the tunnel was dug it was propped up at regular intervals with stakes and beams of wood.

Once the miners were under the walls of the city they put in props, covered them with pitch and oil, and then set fire to them. As the props burned they fell, and when they fell they brought down the roof of the tunnel with them as well as a stretch of the wall immediately overhead. The assaulting infantry then swarmed through the breach.

But the besieger was not the only one to use mines. The besieged could do it too. So there was counter-mining, the kind that was to be repeated by both sides in the 1914-18 War. The besieged garrison built channels across the path of the enemy and màde surprise raids with armed men into his tunnels. Another method was to flood the tunnel by channelling water from the city or a river into it.

Mine detecting

In 189 B.C. the Roman consul, Marcus Fulvius Nobilior, used a great mine at Ambracia (today called Arta) in Epirus. After failing to take the city with mobile towers or by destroying its

Two types of shield used in the Roman army: above, *the circular barma and below,* the rectangular scutum.

The dress of the warriors and priests of ancient Gaul, as reconstructed by Ludovic Menin.

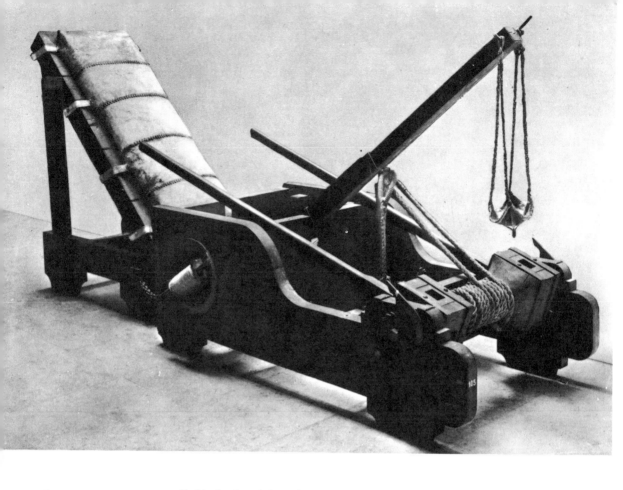

walls (the besieged Aetolians kept building new ones inside) the Romans began to work their mine.

The defenders foresaw the manoeuvre but were unable to pinpoint the exact place chosen by the Romans, so they dug a continuous trench parallel to the city wall, lined it with boards of cedar wood and listened for the vibrations. In this way they discovered the whereabouts of the Roman tunnels and surprised the attackers by countermining. Desperate hand to hand battles followed, but they could not stem the inexorable underground advance of the Romans.

Gas!

The Aetolians then laid underground pipes and through these they blew pitch and sulphur fumes into the Roman tunnels. This was a real attack by asphyxiating gas. It took Marcus Fulvius Nobilior as completely by surprise as the German gas attack at Ypres was to take the French in 1915, and convinced him that he would have to come to terms with such a determined people.

When the city was at last in his hands he let the garrison go free, a most unusual gesture for those days.

The agger

A third method of attack, suited to besiegers as methodical and persistent as the Romans, was the "agger". For all practical purposes this was the kind of embankment recommended by Vitruvius Pollio for defensive purposes. Servius Tullius had a great agger built for the defence of Rome, 28 feet high and 15 feet wide. The agger could be used to bring war machines and mobile towers up to the height of the walls of a besieged city. In other words it was used as a great ramp.

The building of an agger was begun a long way off from the walls to be assaulted. As work progressed emergency palisades were built to protect the men working on the agger. As the work went forward the slope of the agger was raised. By the time it reached the wall it was high enough to allow the attackers to throw bridges from mobile towers onto the walls. Across these bridges the infantry were launched into hand to hand combat with the defenders.

The bottom of the agger was supported by wood and branches. At the siege of Marseilles during the civil war between Caesar and Pompey, Pompey's soldiers managed to destroy the wooden part of Caesar's agger by setting fire to it during a sortie. Caesar's men patiently built another one under the fire and right into the wall—under the noses of the defenders in fact. This one had fixed towers. Caesar's troops assaulted from these towers while mines were set off in the tunnel under the wall.

D. *Terebra, item ex Herone.*

Two drilling machines used to breach the walls of a besieged city.

Two types of agger — ramps used to support siege engines or to bring assault towers up to the enemy walls. The agger on the left is made of beaten earth; the one on the right is constructed of masonry.

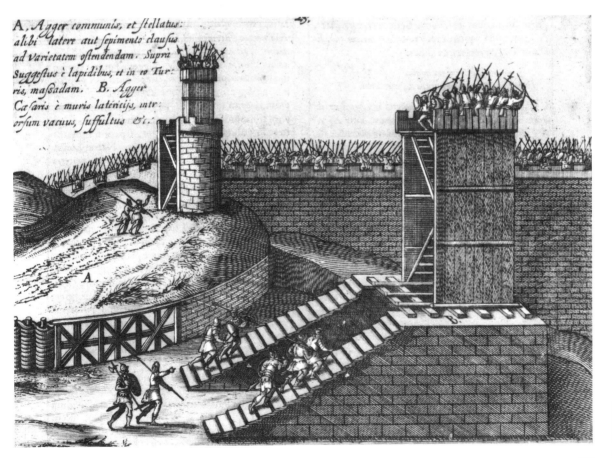

Retreating Gauls destroy their cities and countryside to delay the Roman army.

A model of the siege works constructed by Caesar for the attack on the city of Avaricum. Note the long approach ways made of animal skins and the central bulwark of tree trunks.

west, and in force from the valley of the Seine. The tactics employed by Vercingetorix were simple and exactly right for a struggle against the well-equipped, highly disciplined Roman legions. The tribes avoided meeting the Roman army in the kind of pitched battle that suited them; instead they harassed by guerilla attacks, by the burning of villages in the path of the Romans; by attacking communications and by surprise attacks on small units of Roman cavalry.

Revolt in Gaul

Such were the methods of siege warfare practised in 52 B.C. when Caesar had to push to one side the intricate political problems facing him in Rome and hurry to Gaul to suppress a revolt of the Arverni. It was not the first time that the Gauls had revolted against Roman government and in every case repression had been difficult and bloody.

The standard of revolt was raised by Vercingetorix, the ambitious chief of the Arverni tribe. Immediately other tribes hastened to join him—from the valley of the Loire, from the south

Scorched earth

Vercingetorix called the Gallic chiefs to council and stressed the need to create an empty space around the Romans—the same scorched earth policy that the Russians used against the Germans in the Second World War.

All the chiefs supported such tactics and in one day they burned twenty cities in the fertile region of the Bituriges. But Vercingetorix did not burn Avaricum ("the most beautiful city in Gaul") because he was unable to resist the pleas of the inhabitants who begged him on their knees to spare their beauti-

ful city. They claimed that it was impregnable because of its position surrounded by a river and a marsh with only a single entrance.

Caesar camped in front of this entrance and ordered an agger with two towers to be built there. The nature of the ground prevented the construction of the traditional inner and outer fortified rings. Vercingetorix set up his camp sixteen miles away but later moved closer when he ran out of forage for his animals. His troops were in sullen mood for morale was low and they were beginning to doubt his intentions and ability to carry on the war.

Fire

Meanwhile the Roman agger was moving towards the city. In 25 days despite the bad weather, the soldiers had built it to a height of 80 feet. It was 330 feet wide. At this point it was set on fire by the Gauls who had dug a gully into a tunnel to reach it. They were highly efficient at this kind of work, for as Caesar himself said: "They have extensive iron mines and every type of tunnel is used there".

With the agger alight the Gauls made a sortie from the two city gates, throwing torches, pitch and dry wood and causing the Roman besiegers a moment of uncertainty. Caesar could not help admiring the obstinacy of the Gauls as they attacked one of his towers in successive waves. The tower was already in flames, and the Gauls kept the fire going by throwing balls of tallow and pitch which they passed from hand to hand. One by one the Gauls were struck down by huge arrows fired from the Roman "scorpion" device.

Next day the situation was restored. The sky overhead was dark and the Romans were at work on the "point of approach"—that is the point from which the besiegers would launch their attack.

Escape by night

The spectre of defeat stared the Gauls in the face, and the defenders of Avaricum made the sudden decision to escape by night and try to reach Vercingetorix although they had no idea where he was. The women of the city, terrified, implored the men not to abandon them and their children to the enemy. They began screaming and their screams warned the Romans that the garrison was ready to break out.

This was the moment for action, and in the icy rain of dawn Caesar gave his troops the signal to attack. The legionaries bounded from the towers onto the walls. The Gauls massed in the centre of the city in wedge-shaped formation and stoutly awaited the attack.

But the Romans did not come down from the walls. They held the battlements and thus encircled the defenders who then broke formation in an attempt to escape. They were followed by old people, women and children.

The Roman fury

Suddenly the Roman fury was let loose.

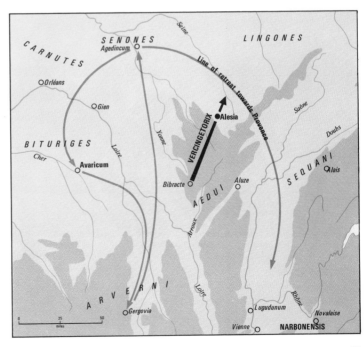

Plan of the campaign conducted by Caesar in Gaul in 52 B.C.

Mount Rea, seen from Alesia. The Gallic cavalry, led by Vercassivellaunus, attacked here in an attempt to break through the Roman encirclement.

Plan of Alesia and surrounding country. The two red lines show the encircling trenches of the Romans.

Blinded by the desire for vengeance, and with no thought of booty, the legionaries attacked without mercy. They ran riot in a terrifying massacre, sparing neither woman nor child. Only 800 survivors reached Vercingetorix out of a population of 40,000. "The most beautiful city in Gaul" had become a cemetery.

This disastrous defeat, and the massacre that followed did not damage the reputation of Vercingetorix as a commander. In fact his reputation was enhanced because, if his advice to burn the city had been followed, all the lives lost would have been saved. He asked for, and was given, reinforcements by the tribal chiefs, but above all he had to find good archers and cavalry.

Caesar stayed at Avaricum for some days and took possession of all the supplies in the city. The soldiers also took with them what they could because they knew they had a long campaign ahead of them. Gergovia, four miles south of Clermont-Ferrand, was a stronghold of the Arverni and it had to be taken if the rebellion was to be destroyed at its heart. It was Vercingetorix's home ground and a focal point of the siege.

Caesar's manoeuvres

Caesar split up his army. Labienus with four legions marched against the Senones and Parisii, the tribes occupying the region where Paris stands today. At that time it was called Lutetia. Caesar, at the head of the other six legions, marched towards Gergovia.

Caesar wanted to win a favourable position for a decisive battle. Firstly he launched a surprise attack that was immediately successful. But his

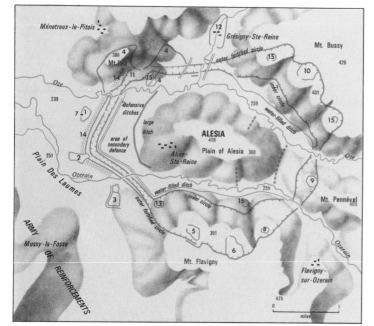

troops, emboldened by success and ignoring their orders, pressed on to the walls of the city and began the assault. The Gauls were prepared for them and repulsed them with great loss. When the Romans fell back they left 700 legionaries dead on the ground.

This setback, serious enough in itself, was to be even more serious in its consequences. The Aedui, the only Gauls still loyal to Rome, went over to the side of the rebels. Vercingetorix, sensing that victory was within reach, increased his demands on the tribes for men.

Vercingetorix besieged

Caesar, finding his communications with Provence and Italy cut, sent for help to the Germanic tribes and obtained their support. Then he retreated with his army towards Provence. Vercingetorix decided to attack the legions with his cavalry, but his attack was beaten off and he had to take refuge in the city of Alesia with 80,000 troops.

This retreat placed him in a desperate situation. With all these extra mouths to feed the grain reserves of Alesia would be exhausted in a little over 30 days. His first step was to get rid of his cavalry, the spearhead of all his attacks. He sent them away by night in great secrecy and asked each man to return with additional soldiers and supplies as soon as possible.

The summer of the year 52 B.C. was drawing to a close. Caesar, learning of the situation in Alesia from deserters and prisoners, gave orders for a siege.

Fortified rings

This time the nature of the ground allowed for the two fortified circles to be constructed around the city. The inner was eleven miles in circumference, the outer fourteen miles.

In addition to these Caesar ordered a ditch about fifteen feet deep and wide to be dug around the city. About 130 yards outside it ran the inner circle of the defence. Round this another ditch, of the same depth and width, was dug, and this was filled with water diverted from a nearby river. Between the ditches he placed traps and obstacles, pits were filled with pointed stakes, and wooden blades and pegs with iron

Model of a section of the Roman trench lines surrounding Alesia. On the right can be seen the defensive agger with a guard tower. On the left, facing open country, a double line of trenches protects the investing army against relief forces approaching the city. The trenches are further protected by pits containing pointed stakes and barbed spikes.

A reconstruction of a battle scene during the siege of Alesia, by the French painter Henri Motte (late 19th century). All siege engines and weapons are accurately portrayed down to the smallest detail.

A coin portraying Commius, Gallic ally of Vercingetorix.

hooks attached were stuck into the ground.

A little more than 100 yards from the inner ring was the layout of the outer ring, also surrounded on its outer side by a six foot ditch. In that circle a month's supply of provisions was stored.

Reinforcements

Meanwhile Gaul had responded readily to the request of Vercingetorix for more men. According to Caesar 8,000 cavalry and 250,000 infantry were on the march towards Alesia under the command of Commius. With such a large army at their disposal the Gauls were certain of victory but an army of this size could not move quickly and Vercingetorix was already in difficulty in Alesia.

Differences of opinion developed among his counsellors. There were those who talked of surrender, and

those determined to resist to the last, eating old people and children if they had to. At this stage a huge Gallic army arrived and took up a position around the outer circle of the Roman defence. From Alesia the exultant citizens ran out and many fell into the first ditch of the Roman defence.

The Roman attack

Caesar wasted no time now. Every soldier was assigned to his post and given his instructions. The cavalry was ordered out to the attack at midday. At sunset Caesar's German cavalry launched the decisive charge. The Gallic cavalry and the archers who depended on it for cover fell in large numbers.

The citizens withdrew within the city walls again, their hopes dashed.

A night and day passed and then Commius's army attacked the outer circle of the Roman defences, making enough noise to be heard in Alesia.

Vercingetorix was not asleep, nor was any person in Alesia that night. The city gates were thrown open and trumpet blasts summoned the citizens to the battle.

The Roman infantry defending the outer front used missiles of all sorts, but these had little effect in the dark. This is where the traps were useful. The cries of agonized soldiers filled the air. The attack faltered and the attackers retreated in panic. Silence fell again and the Gauls inside the first ditch realized there was nothing else to be done except go back inside the city and wait.

Army of Commius arrives

They did not have to wait long. About nine o'clock the next night Commius sent 60,000 picked men under Vercassivellaunus towards a hill which the Romans had not been able to include in their fortification. It was guarded by two legions—about 12,000 men. Vercassivellaunus spent the night in hiding behind the hill and about midday attacked the Roman position. At the same time the cavalry rode up to the outer ring of the Roman fortification and the rest of the Gallic army formed into battle order.

From Alesia Vercingetorix saw this movement and, guessing what the plan was, ordered his troops out. Now they were attacking everywhere and the Romans were forced to run back and forth along the great circle to reinforce their defences.

The attack by Vercassivellaunus was the more dangerous. His men pressed it home with great vigour and, having filled the trenches and traps with anything lying to hand, could now run over them safely.

Caesar intervenes

Caesar sent Labienus with six cohorts (about 3,000 men) to this part of the front, then intervened in person in a sector where the men from Alesia had reached a part of the inner fortifications.

Having rectified the situation there, he ordered the cavalry outside the outer circle to outflank the enemy. Then he rejoined Labienus who was making desperate efforts to hold off the enemy. The Gauls recognized Caesar by the scarlet cloak that he was wearing and which he always wore in battle. The clamour rose and the fighting became more intense. The Romans dropped their javelins and drew their swords. Then suddenly the Roman cavalry fell on the rear of the Gauls, and other cohorts arrived from sectors not being threatened.

The Gauls, taken by surprise, fled and were slaughtered by the cavalry in the pursuit. Vercassivellaunus himself was taken prisoner. Seventy-four Gallic standards were piled up at Caesar's feet.

The whole of Commius's army panicked, broke and fled. The Roman infantry were too tired to follow and there was no pursuit by the cavalry until midnight when there was only a rearguard still in contact.

Alesia falls

Vercingetorix was already back inside Alesia, his dream of a free Gaul destroyed. Next day the king of the Arverni talked with his counsellors. There was no way out for any of them. The king, to placate the Romans, could either die at the hands of his counsellors or give himself up alive and trust his life to Caesar.

Emissaries were sent to discuss surrender. Caesar demanded the surrender of arms and leaders. He was seated in a trench when he saw Vercingetorix approaching, unarmed and defeated.

Vercingetorix was sent to Rome as a prisoner and allowed to live for six more years. He was executed in 46 B.C.

After the fall of Alesia, Vercingetorix surrenders to Caesar — an illustration by Ludovic Pogliaghi for Bertolini's History of Italy.

CHAPTER 4

THE CRUSADES

In order to understand why the Crusades began, we have to look at the history of the period. In the 7th century A.D. the Arab people, exalted by the prophecies of Mohammed, who promised them that any man who died fighting for his faith would go to heaven, began the period of expansion that was to carry them on an invincible wave through the whole of North Africa and into Spain and even France.

A nation formerly of shepherds and caravan drivers became an invincible army that transformed the Mediterranean world. They created an enormous empire, from Asia Minor to Spain, that was to endure for three centuries.

Arab expansion

The Arabs set no limit to their expansion. It was set for them. They were stopped at Constantinople in 717 by the Roman Emperor of the East, Leo III, called the Isaurian. The French invasion was halted by Charles the Hammer at the battle of Poitiers in 732. Following this battle, the Arabs withdrew to the Spanish side of the Pyrenees, so France escaped the Moorish occupation that was to be the fate of Spain.

Halted on land, the Arabs continued their offensive at sea. They occupied Crete about 828. Between 826 and 902 they captured Sicily and established themselves along the Mediterranean coastline of Europe—in Corsica, Sardinia, Southern Italy and in Provence.

It is a notable fact that the conquerors were tolerant of the Christian religion and a fact of history that they left Spain a Christian country. It is also a matter of history that the Franks of the Crusader states had friendly relations with the Moslems, which was a constant surprise to crusading zealots from Western Europe when they arrived.

Spain revolts

European revolt against the Arab conquests began in Spain, where Aragon, Leonó and Castile became independent kingdoms. They carried on the war of liberation which became an anti-Moslem fight under the leadership of Rodrigo Diaz of Bivar, known as *El Cid* or *El Campeador*, who died in 1099.

The wave of revolt spread along the entire Mediterranean and the Italian maritime republics were in the forefront of the insurrection, especially Genoa, Pisa and Amalfi.

In the east, the Byzantine Empire regained Crete in 960. Between 963 and 969, Cyprus and Antioch were retaken. Everything seemed to promise complete success to the Christians. Then they suffered two severe reverses which served as warnings. In 1071 a Turkish army defeated the Byzantines at Manzikert, taking their emperor Romanus IV a prisoner. At Zalaca in Spain, the Moslem army destroyed the Christian

View of the Mediterranean from the window of a castle built by the Crusaders at Byblos (Beirut).

forces of King Alphonso VI of Castile.

Turks as leaders

One thing has to be noted here—Turks, not Arabs, were the leaders of the Moslem world and controlled the Moslem empire. In the 10th century, the Turks had served the Arabs as slaves, mercenaries and officials, then Turks invaded the Arab lands in force and became the masters. Some time in the 11th century, probably later than earlier, power passed from the Arab caliphs to the Turkish emirs.

The Christian world now realized that their partial victories against the Turks were of no real account. In order to remove the threat posed by Islam, its military power had to be met by an equally unified force.

Peter the Hermit (1050-1115), the French preacher who, according to legend, roused the Christians of Europe to "take up the Cross" in the First Crusade. In actual fact his preaching was limited to northern France and south-west Germany.

The Holy War

The initiative in this came from Pope Urban II who, in the course of the councils of Clermont in France, between March and November 1095, pleaded for a holy war. His pleas were strengthened by the fact that Moslem forces now stood astride all the pilgrim routes followed by Christians travelling from Western Europe to the Holy Land. His pleas were answered with equal fervour,

the response of the people being "God wills it".

This was the beginning of the great popular movement that was to become known to history as the Crusades.

There is no doubt that the preaching of a holy war or a holy crusade fell on receptive ears and that most people were genuinely and sincerely concerned about the fate of the holy places in Jerusalem. But we have to realize that the underlying causes of the Crusades, which induced people to "take up the Cross" and join a military force to fight a dangerous war in distant lands, were more complex than simply concern for pilgrims or holy places. They were also political and later, as we shall see, the great feudal lords used them as a pretext for plunder.

Unruly mob

In 1096, Peter the Hermit and Walter the Penniless led an unruly mob of fanatics through Germany, Hungary and Bulgaria and crossed the Bosphorus. This mob had as its aim the recovery of Jerusalem and the destruction of the infidels. They were annihilated by a Turkish army at Nicaea.

This first Crusade has passed into history as "the Lunatics' Crusade" and was the lunatic forerunner of the eight subsequent expeditions described by history as Crusades.

Early Crusades

The early Crusades were made up of devoted men sincerely dedicated to liberating the Sepulchre of Christ. This fervour and sense of purpose gradually weakened and eventually was lost altogether, submerged in the game of self-interest and the feudal thirst for power.

Most of the Crusaders came from France, Normandy, Brittany and England. The German contribution was slight, at least until the Second Crusade. The Germans arrived late on the scene,

كتذى ودخى مجموع اصحاب ياتيله يراغله عزم ايلديلر

اندن يوله كرديلر كتذلرپس تقدير ربانى وامر
سبحانى انوك كبى ولديپكم يولده اول لشكر كيدركن

This old Persian miniature shows Mohammed (bottom left with his face veiled) guiding the Islamic army in his holy war.

because the Emperor was involved in his struggle with the Papacy and with risings against his authority by the free communes.

From 1147 to 1149, Conrad III, leader of the Germanic States, took part with a large army, in the Second Crusade. Richard, Coeur de Lion, king of England joined the Crusaders in 1191 with an army of 4,000 men-at-arms and 4,000 foot soldiers.

The Christian allies

The crusading army suffered from the defects common to any army made up of a number of allies of different nations. The different contingents had little in common with each other. Their customs were different and they spoke different languages. In fact, the crusading army was not an army in the real sense of the term but an aggregate of individual

The siege of Jerusalem, from a 14th century Flemish painting. Although this painting depicts an incident in A.D. 70, during the conquest of Jerusalem by Tipi, the weapons and fortifications are medieval.

forces, each fighting its own war in its own way.

Many such contingents opted out as soon as they had acquired a new state and settled down after reaching agreement with the local Turkish forces. After withdrawing from the war, they were careful to preserve their position as conquerors and did business with the local merchants. Their relationship with their Moslem neighbours was good, and they did not want to be disturbed in their enjoyment of the softness and refinements of oriental life.

The Christian Knights

This weakening of the crusading spirit did not apply to certain religious military orders. These orders were voluntary associations of men determined to preserve the original purpose and dignity of the Crusades. Their aim was a simple one—to free the Sepulchre of Christ, by armed intervention, from Moslem control.

The most famous of these orders was the order of the Knights Hospitallers (otherwise known as Knights of St John and later Knights of Malta), the Knights Templar and the Teutonic Knights. Their organization was very strict and their rules severe—the Templars, for example, were obliged to sleep in their armour, to fight to the death and to refrain from hunting for sport unless the quarry were lions.

Fortresses bar the way

The first Crusaders were almost helpless against the walls of the enemy fortresses and quickly realized that they were faced with siege warfare of a kind they were not equipped to carry out. All the equipment needed for the kind of siege facing them had been left at home. They had, therefore, to use whatever the Byzantine emperor Alexius could spare, build from scratch, improvize, or invent new equipment of their own.

The Crusaders had also to build barracks to house their garrisons, and all their camp followers. Because of the different climate they could not build the kind of castles they had at home; the building materials had to be of local origin; and the methods of attack likely to be employed against them would be strange.

For example, there was no point in using wood as roofing material or for the construction of outside walls, because the Turks were adept at the use of "Greek fire"—incendiary material blown from tubes by means of bellows and in principle rather like the flame-throwers used by modern armies.

Siege and counter-siege

During the wars, the Crusaders conducted sieges and were in turn besieged. The most important of these took place during the First Crusade at Nicaea in

1097. Several cities of great historical importance bore this name. One was in Corsica, another was on the Côte D'Azur on the site of what is now Nice. A third was in Greece near the famous pass of Thermopylae.

The one that concerns us in this chapter is the Nicaea of Bithynia and it is the most important of all in the present context. It still exists under the name of Iznik and lies on the eastern shore of Lake Iznik in North Turkey, about sixty miles from Istanbul (Byzantium).

Nicaea was part of the Roman Empire of the East and two important ecumenical councils were held there—in 325 at the time of Constantine, and in 787. It was part of the Empire almost up to the time of the Crusades. But the Seljuk Turks had captured it and the Byzantine emperor, Alexius, saw the Crusades as the best way of getting it back. In exchange for assistance from the Crusaders he promised to supply them with food and weapons as well as ships to cross the Bosphorus at the start of the expedition.

The armies of the Crusaders arrived from every part of Europe, joined up in Byzantium in 1096, and remained there until April 1097. On 15th May, they attacked Nicaea.

Attack on Nicaea

The attacking forces numbered per-perhaps 35,000 fighting men, but they had no overall commander although legend has it that they were led by Godfrey of Bouillon. He was, in fact, commander of only part of the force.

Two examples of the Crusaders' military architecture. On the left the castle at Byblos. Like so many Crusaders' castles, this one was built on ancient foundations – the walls in the foreground date back to 2700 B.C. On the right a tower of the castle at Sidon whose walls are reinforced by marble columns taken from Greek and Roman temples.

Lack of co-ordination resulting from split command meant that the operation lasted much longer than anyone had expected.

A decision was taken to use mines, and twenty minelayers approached the city walls under the protection of wooden shields. They attacked the base of the walls with pickaxes and were buried under a shower of stones. It was an unknown Italian who solved the problem.

He built a tower at a considerable angle from the vertical which was placed against the walls. The missiles thrown down by the defenders slid down the sloping surface to the foot of the tower. Meanwhile some of the men were working with picks to open up a vertical breach in the wall and others were working below with mines. The walls gave way suddenly, sweeping the miners away with them. The city now lay open to attack.

Surrender to Turks

But the attack never came. Alexius, knowing full well that the Crusaders would loot and burn the city, had secretly arranged its surrender with the Turks, and he garrisoned Nicaea with Turkish mercenaries. His action enraged the Frankish Crusaders who had intended to loot the town. When Godfrey of Bouillon set off with his army across the plain of Anatolia, Alexius sent only a token force along with him. He was more concerned about reconquering his empire.

Slow march

The Crusaders' march across Asia Minor was slow and difficult. They won the battle of Dorylaeum on 1st July, 1097, and four months later they reached Antioch, one of the most beautiful cities of the ancient world.

Antioch stood on the banks of the river Oronte and the surrounding marshes. The Crusaders formed up on the left bank of the river. To reach the walls, they would have to bridge the river and establish a bridgehead on the other side.

Help for the besieged Turkish garrison, in the form of Moslem troops, arrived from Aleppo, Caesarea and Damascus. The Crusaders fought a pitched battle and routed them. Two thousand Turkish soldiers lost their lives. The Crusaders cut off the heads of two hundred Turkish soldiers and threw them over the walls of Antioch. It was a horrifying but useless warning. The city did not surrender.

Lack of food

The Crusaders failed to capture Antioch. Its beautiful walls, as wide as its roads and guarded by four hundred towers, defied every assault.

All the crusading army could do was compete with the Turks in barbarity. They continued to throw the heads of Moslem prisoners over the city walls on which stood stakes bearing the heads of Christian captives.

In that year, 1097, the beautiful and fertile countryside around Antioch was stripped bare by the Crusaders who were living off the land. Having used up all the food stocks, the Crusaders had by Christmas reached the point of starvation, and there were even reports of cannibalism among them.

Antioch the prize

At a war council the feudal Crusader lords were addressed by the Norman prince Bohemund of Tarentum who was, in the military sense, the most competent of the Christian captains. He posed the question of Antioch as war booty and proposed that the city should be awarded to whichever captain took it with his own force.

This suggestion was contrary to pledges which had been given earlier to Alexius and someone recalled that at Byzantium the Crusaders had undertaken, on oath, to hand the city over to Alexius who was its legitimate sovereign.

Bohemund reacted to this reminder by stating that he had no more money, that his men were tired, and that he was therefore going to leave the camp and return to Europe. Such was his prestige that the council changed its mind and agreed with his proposals. Antioch would go to whoever succeeded in conquering it.

Massacre

Naturally, the rôle of conqueror fell to Bohemund himself who had detailed plans ready for the capture of the city. He had made certain of the collaboration of a traitor, an Armenian named Firuz, whom the Turks had entrusted with the defence of three towers. On the night of 3rd June, 1098, Bohemund's

The glacis, or sloping bank, of a medieval castle during a siege. Two throwing engines can be seen – a multiple-shot catapult on the tower and, in the foreground to the right, a counter-weighted trebuchet ready for action. When the counter-weight was released, the missile was thrown a great distance.

55

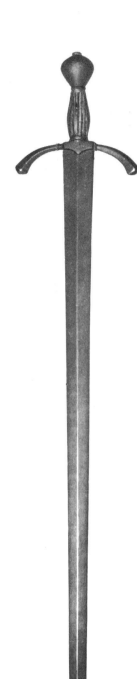

men hoisted their ladders at these towers and entered the city.

A great massacre took place, followed by a thorough sacking of the city. Everything was destroyed except one citadel in the heart of the city, garrisoned by a single Saracen division. In an attempt to capture this remaining stronghold, Bohemund himself was wounded.

The jubilation of the Crusaders lasted only a few days. The gates of the city, which they had opened, had suddenly to be closed again. On the horizon appeared an army of the Caliph Kerbogha, arriving too late to save Antioch from destruction.

Rôles reversed

Now a new siege began with the rôles completely reversed. The Crusaders were the besieged and the Turks the besiegers. The first thing Kerbogha did was to destroy all communication lines to the sea, to prevent the arrival of Byzantine reinforcements.

On 8th June, the Crusaders opened one of the city gates and rushed out to the attack. The attack was repulsed and the Crusaders beaten back. During the rush to re-enter the city, many of them perished by suffocation and trampling.

The situation, already serious, became desperate when plague broke out. The Crusaders were now trapped between the Saracens in the citadel and Kerbogha's investing Turks. They were reduced to drinking the blood of their horses. Many Crusaders deserted. Letting themselves down from the walls with ropes during the night they escaped through the Turkish lines to join up with the Emperor Alexius, who was marching on Antioch with reinforcements.

The sword reputed to belong to Godfrey of Bouillon, Duke of Lorraine, one of the most famous of the crusading knights.

Enter St Andrew

At this point in the story legend intrudes, as it was to do in modern times at Mons in 1914. A certain Pierre Barthelemy, chaplain to the army of Raymund de Saint-Gilles, Count of Toulouse, declared that he had seen St Andrew in a dream. St Andrew had revealed to him that the spear which had pierced Christ's rib on the Cross was in Antioch. He was to find it and hand it over to his leaders, because whoever used it in battle would be invincible.

Overcoming all their doubts and hesitations, the Crusaders dug in the place the Saint had indicated and there they found the head of a lance. Enthusiasm knew no bounds and on 28th June, with the sacred spear at the head of the army, the Crusaders tried again to make a sortie.

This time they had a single commander, recognized as such, Bohemund. The Turkish camp, on the other hand, was rent by discord. Many of the emirs had deserted Kerbogha when the two armies met. Kerbogha, his forces weakening, was defeated and his archers dispersed and killed.

When the Turks in the citadel saw what had happened they too sur-

Digging a mine during a medieval siege. The sappers work in a tunnel protected by a shelter of tree trunks. They are attempting to undermine the walls so that they will collapse.

rendered. The emir in command of the citadel requested one of the Crusader's flags to put up as a sign of surrender. He was given the flag of Raymund de Saint-Gilles, Count of Toulouse, but Bohemund's men soon tore it down and hoisted their own leader's flag in its place. So Antioch went to Bohemund.

Bohemund thus established the second Frankish state in the east and in so doing further alienated the Greeks with whom the Pope had hoped to reach a friendly settlement.

On to Jerusalem

The march of the Crusaders towards the Holy City of Jerusalem was held up by two further sieges—that at Marra, which capitulated on 11th December, 1098, and that of Arca, which had to be abandoned on 13th May, 1099. Both sieges resulted in more starvation, more quarrels and more massacres.

Before the siege of Arca, the sacred spear again enters the stage. This spear which, according to legend, contributed so much to the victory at Antioch was still in the possession of Raymund de Saint-Gilles. Many people now hated this man who remained obstinately faithful to Alexius and prevented the various feudal units from sacking and taking possession of the towns they conquered. Intent on damaging his reputation, his opponents put it about that he had invented the story of the sacred spear for his own personal advantage. For eight months the Crusaders wrangled over this and finally the barbarism of the Middle Ages triumphed. The chaplain Pierre Barthelemy was to be subjected to trial by fire.

Christians scaling the walls of Jerusalem — a 15th century Flemish miniature from History of the Crusades.

Ordeal by fire

Twigs and dry olive branches, laid in a long line, were set alight. If Pierre could walk across the flames unharmed, the authenticity of the relic could no longer be doubted.

Barefooted, Pierre walked through the fire. After his ordeal, he was left in the care of Raymund. He died twelve days later from burns.

"Count Raymund", says a chronicler of the time, "kept the spear for a long time after that, then he lost it; I don't know how."

Between August and September 1098, the Fatimite caliph had taken Jerusalem from his co-religionists, the Selguichidean Turks (so-called after Seljuk their mythical ancestor), who had conquered Palestine twenty years earlier. Therefore, it was up to the Fatimites to defend Jerusalem, the final goal of the Crusaders.

According to the Genoese chronicler Caffaro, himself a Crusader, the Christians found the water tanks outside the city of Jerusalem destroyed so that they had to draw water from the River Jordan.

Massacre again

The siege had been in progress for about one month when William Embriaco and his brother Primus arrived at Jaffa with two galleys. On landing, they destroyed the galleys as they did not want them to fall into the hands of the Saracens of Ascalona.

The wood from the ships was to be used to build the siege machinery necessary for taking Jerusalem and it was transported there. The Christians, overjoyed by the arrival of Genoese reinforcements, welcomed them warmly.

Using their timber, the Genoese built the siege machinery and within forty days the city capitulated. The usual massacre followed and in this case defending Moslems and resident Jews were killed indiscriminately. The date was 15th July, 1099, and on that date the first crusade can be said to have ended.

The Christians enter Jerusalem at the end of their long and bloody advance across Asia Minor and Palestine. In the centre is Peter the Hermit who rejoined the crusading army after deserting it at the siege of Antioch.

Count Baldwin, brother of Godfrey of Bouillon, is crowned king of the new
Crusader state by the Patriarch of Jerusalem, another 15th century
Flemish miniature from History of the Crusades.

CHAPTER 5

CONSTANTINOPLE

A curious Turkish weapon – a trident used by the infantry. The bearer's hand and forearm were protected by armour.

Constantinople, capital of the Roman Empire of the East, fell to the Turks on 29th May, 1453. The event, in the view of some historians, marks the end of the period we call the Middle Ages.

Formerly Byzantium, Constantinople was named the new capital of the Roman Empire by Constantine the Great in A.D. 330. The city had an ancient history, having first been settled by the Greeks in the 7th and 8th centuries B.C., and had become the heart of the old Byzantine Empire. Constantine probably chose it because of its strategic position and economic importance. He had the city rebuilt in grand style and added monuments and treasures brought from other famous cities—Alexandria in Egypt, Ephesus, Antioch, Athens and even Rome itself.

Situated at the mouth of the straits of the Bosphorus the city dominated communications between the east with its luxury goods and the west with its commercial products. Its strategic position was exploited for profit, revenue being derived from toll-bridges and the transit duties imposed on the merchants.

East meets West

Constantinople was a crucible of cultures, a meeting place of many races, a melting pot of ideas. The culture of Greece, which was the basis and character of the old Byzantine civilization, here came face to face with the new cultures of Rome and of the Orient.

Little by little oriental ways began to dominate. Religious differences grew into disputes and disputes even between Christians grew.

Greek philosophy played a part in this. The devotion to speculative thought increased religious strife. Everywhere were representations of Christ. His effigy was even on coinage circulating as far as India and bearing the inscription "Christos Basileus"—Christ the Emperor. The Evangelist occupied a throne by the side of the Emperor and every dogma of the Christian faith was discussed, not with love, but with fierce hatred.

The great schism

Christ was thrust aside in the wrangles over Christianity. Inevitably there was a split in the Church—a great schism between the Roman Church on the one hand and the Greek Church on the other: that is between Catholicism and Orthodoxy. This schism has lasted until the present time.

Inside the city were Turkish adherents of the Christian faith as well as Roman Catholic and Greek Orthodox adherents. They were constantly arguing among themselves despite the religious union between Rome and Constantinople established at the Council of Florence between 1438 and 1445. The actual decree of unity had been issued on 6th July, 1439.

Mortars used by the Turks in the assault on Constantinople in 1453 can still be seen at the fortress of Rumeli Hisar, one of the key points of the siege.

Sieges and battles

Because of its strategic importance
Constantinople was a major objective
in war, and it was many times besieged.

In 559 it had to defend itself against
the assault of Huns and Slavs. Arab
armies attacked it from 673 to 678 and
from 717 to 718. It was besieged by the
Crusaders who conquered it in 1204.
In 1261 it was besieged by the Byzantines themselves and reconquered. The
Turks then attacked Constantinople in
1453 and its subsequent fall was a
turning point in world history.

By 1326 the Turks had succeeded in
creating a Moslem state in the northern
part of Anatolia, the capital of which
was Brusa. Five years later they occupied Nicaea and in 1356 they took
over Thrace in Gallipoli, thanks to an
earthquake that had destroyed the

walls of the city. In 1361 they took
Adrianople and in 1371, after the
battle of Maritza, they occupied Bulgaria. In 1389, after bloody massacres,
they became masters of Serbia and
the following year the Turkish army
stood along the Danube.

Decline of the Roman Empire

The great Roman Empire of the East
had been swallowed up by Turkish
expansion except for Constantinople
and the little of its surrounding territory—Thessalonika (Salonika) and the
Peloponnese. But it had been tottering
before then.

In actual fact Serbs and Bulgarians
had nearly always managed to avoid its
domination as had the principalities
and Frankish dominions in most of
Greece and the archipelago. In Con-

stantinople itself colonies of Venetian and Genoese merchants technically recognized Roman sovereignty but were never troubled by it, and Roman power was not enforced.

Indeed the Empire was in such a state of decay that in 1423 the Governor of Thessalonika could sell his city to the Venetians whom he considered more capable of defending it. But seven years later the Thessalonikans fell under the Turkish onslaught.

Western indifference

Curiously enough, the countries of western Europe watched the decline and fall of the old Roman Empire with total indifference, completely unaware of its significance and gravity.

John V (Palaeologus), who reigned from 1341 to 1391, was deposed three times and restored to his throne three times. This was the saddest period in the history of Constantinople. John turned to Rome and Venice for help, but in vain; and it was only during the reign of Manuel II, his son, that Europe at last sent an army to the Balkans.

This army from Europe was defeated by the Turks at Nicopolis in 1396. Constantinople was then under siege by the Turks but did not fall.

Tamerlane

It was saved by the great Tamerlane (the Tatar Timur) who routed the Turkish sultan Bajazet and reconquered a great part of Anatolia. Bajazet was defeated by Tamerlane near Ankara on 20th July, 1402. He was captured there and died the following year at Ag Shetir.

Tamerlane's campaign had thrust back the Turkish wave for the time being. The defeat of Bajazet, if it had been followed by decisive action, could have led to a Turkish evacuation of Europe. But the Roman Empire had

not the forces and western Europe refused to give help despite the fact that Manuel II had gone as far as Paris and London in search of allies.

Around 1413 the Empire, built up on the conquests of Tamerlane, collapsed and the Turks were again on the offensive.

Manuel meanwhile had abdicated in favour of his son, John VIII. In the hope of obtaining support from the west John VIII used his imperial authority to force union between the churches— the union which had been decided by the

The great French soldier Jean Le Meingre, called Bouciquaut, compels the Turks to raise the siege of Constantinople in 1399; another incident which illustrates how powerless the Byzantine empire had become.

Council of Florence and incited such hatred and strife among the Byzantines.

In the meantime the Hungarian army which had driven the Turks out of Sofia in 1443 was in turn defeated by them at Varna in 1444. The Hungarian king, Wladislaus, was killed in the battle.

Christian alliance

The Hungarian regent János Hunyadi then formed an alliance of Christian princes and moved with a joint army against the Turks. In the second battle of Kossovo on 19th October, 1448, his army too was defeated. The Roman

Sultan Mohammed II (1430-1481), depicted on a small medal attributed to Matthew Pasti. Called "the Conqueror" or "the Great", he was a fearless warrior but of inhuman ferocity.

Empire of the East was now dead in all but name.

On the morning of 5th April, 1453, the inhabitants of Constantinople were called to the city's walls by trumpeters and drummers. From there they saw a terrifying spectacle—a great Turkish army in battle array from the Sea of Marmara to the Golden Horn.

The Turkish army

There has been much argument about the size of this Turkish force. According to some historians, such as Ducas, the Byzantine who lived at the time of the siege, it was made up of half a million men. Others put it as low as 80,000

men. Whatever its size, it was a formidable force greedy for booty. Probably it numbered 80,000 men plus irregular troops, and at their mercy lay the beautiful weakened city, last outpost of the once proud Roman Empire.

At the head of this army stood a famous and ruthless sovereign—Mohammed II. He was a young man of 21, dedicated to extending Turkish domination in Europe, and so crowning the work of the earlier sultans by the conquest of Constantinople.

Mohammed II v Constantine XI

His was a complex personality. Highly cultured, he was also ambitious and energetic to the point of ferocity. Opposite him, at the head of the Byzantine army, was Constantine Palaeologus with ten years' experience of government.

Constantine was a man of great gifts and strong character and was undoubtedly one of the best emperors the Byzantines had ever had. But at his command he had only a small army with which to oppose Mohammed; an army of no more than seven thousand men, the wretched remnants of the great host of 100,000 soldiers that had once made up the imperial force.

Constantine's fleet, which had once numbered seven hundred ships, was now reduced to twenty-six serviceable craft. Latterly his army of seven thousand obtained a reinforcement of three thousand Italian mercenaries and volunteers from Pisa, Venice and Genoa.

The Genoese, about seven hundred in all, tried a few sorties in the early days of the siege but soon had to abandon all idea of offensive attack because of the large numbers opposing them.

The city's defences

The defences of Constantinople were laid out in an impressive system of

concentric walls. The city itself followed the triangular shape of the peninsula between the Sea of Marmara and the gulf known as the Golden Horn.

The outermost defences had been built in the 5th century by the emperor Theodosius II. The wall protecting the peninsula on the landward side was five miles in length. It had seven gates and about fifty defence towers.

Near the Aurea Gate a castle with seven towers linked this defensive belt with the wall defending the city on the coastal side. This wall was also reinforced by towers along its whole stretch of seven miles.

In the Middle Ages this would have been a formidable defence system. It would have remained so in the 15th century if there had been inside the city a force sufficient to man the defences. In fact, the Byzantines could man the defences at a density of no more than one man to every five yards of wall.

At any one moment they could increase this density but guards had to be changed and men had to sleep.

Artillery - "God of War"

The disproportion between the artillery of the two sides was also very great. The Turkish artillery was composed exclusively of guns. The Byzantines had some modern cannon but their weapons for the most part were catapults and missiles practically identical to those used in the time of Alexander the Great centuries before.

A further threat to the defence was posed by two castles that had been built by the Turks on the eastern outlet of the Bosphorus. One was on the European shore and another on the opposite shore. They had been built for the express purpose of preventing the passage of ships from the Black Sea to Constantinople. The city was

Constantinople – an 18th century topographical map. On the right can be seen the peninsula of Galata across which Mohammed had his ships dragged.

thus cut off to seaward. In addition to this, the range of the guns in one of the castles, Rumeli-Hisar, could reach the centre of the city.

Defensive chains

Defending the centre of the city on the Golden Horn side were great iron chains stretching across the entrance to the gulf from the walls to the tower of Galata. This barrier prevented Turkish ships from penetrating through the Golden Horn and bombarding Constantinople from that side.

The Turkish fleet, in any case, although large, was made up of weak

Turkish camp during a battle. A wounded soldier is receiving first aid.

units and was unable to prevent five great Genoese vessels loaded with reinforcements from reaching the city. The defenders lowered the chain barrier to allow these ships through, and they were then able to join up with the Byzantine fleet of eight warships and twenty smaller vessels, galleys and boats.

Food and water

Food supplies were no problem for the defenders. Inside the walls they had large numbers of livestock as well as grain and other foodstuffs requisitioned earlier from the surrounding countryside. Water was stored in five huge tanks so the defenders did not have to depend on supplies from the 4th century aqueduct built by the emperor Valens.

One of the great storage tanks, known as the Cisterna Basilica, was a true work of art; 140 yards long, 70 yards wide and supported by 336 pillars placed in twelve rows.

Many of the citizens actively cooperated in the defence of their city, but as they were only part-time soldiers and amateurs they were of little real help. The majority of the 50,000 inhabitants roamed the streets in fear or took refuge in the churches. This was a small population compared with the million people who had inhabited the city in the 8th century.

A monstrous cannon

Mohammed II, recognizing the strength of the city's defences, brought up special siege artillery. He had one huge cannon, gigantic indeed for its time, a real monster made of bronze with a barrel 26 feet eight inches long. This monster hurled missiles of 96 inches calibre and weighing 1,320 pounds. It required 60 oxen to pull and two hundred men to operate it. It was such a specialized piece that the operators had to be specially trained to work it. It took two months to bring it from Adrianople to Constantinople.

Using this cannon in conjunction with the rest of his artillery, Mohammed subjected Constantinople to a bombardment the like of which had never before been seen. Tremendous breaches were blasted in the walls which the defenders could not repair.

Infantry attack

The Turkish infantry was let loose on 18th April but was repulsed. Discouraged, Mohammed II proposed a treaty, an offer he had first made before the siege began. The suggestion was that, in case of surrender, the city would be saved and the emperor allowed to retire to reign in the Peloponnese.

But Constantine made it clear to Mohammed that there could be no talk of surrender and that the defenders were determined to resist to the end. Mohammed then dealt the most spectacular stroke of the siege.

As his ships could not break through by sea because of the chain, he would take them overland.

Land ships

The Turkish troops therefore built a road across the peninsula of Galata, a distance of five miles. The road no longer exists and its route has never been established. But it was built, and

along it on 21st/22nd April, 1453, thousands of men and hundreds of oxen dragged 70 galleys loaded on wooden rollers lubricated with grease.

This tactic was not new. In 1439 the Venetians had crossed from the Adige to Lake Garda in this way across the pass of Torbole.

It was a Venetian, Barbaro, who left a vivid description of the Turkish fleet with its sails hoisted and its oarsmen in place, passing through fields of corn and vineyards and then going down to the Golden Horn. When the sails appeared on the waters of the gulf, the city realized it was lost.

The defenders tried to set fire to the Turkish ships by sending fireships among them but one of the sailors betrayed them and the Turks were able to avoid disaster by destroying the Christian galleys with their cannon.

After the fall of the city, Mohammed's bodyguard camped beneath this tree, called the "tree of the janissaries".

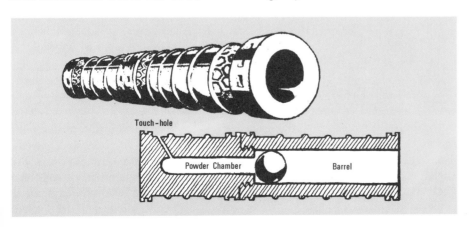

Touch-hole

Powder Chamber   Barrel

The great cannon used by Mohammed in the attack on Constantinople.

Section of the wall between the gates of Poliandrus and San Romano, as it is today. It was here that Constantine Palaeologus, the last Byzantine emperor, fell fighting.

Failure

Meanwhile other infantry attacks had been launched but they met with the same failure as the attack in April. Giustiniani in command of the Genoese, was always there, alert and invincible.

On 25th May, Mohammed made new offers of a treaty to the Emperor but again Constantine adamantly refused to surrender.

But Constantinople had now lost its fleet. Along with the Byzantine ships, the Genoese and Venetian craft had also been destroyed. Mohammed II then had built across the sea a bridge which was supported by enormous barrels. The city was now surrounded in a tight ring.

Religious strife

Inside the city, despite the threat from outside, religious strife between Catholics and Orthodox had flared again. It was an absurd situation in face of the common danger. Orthodox confessors even denied absolution to soldiers who had had any contact with Catholics, or who had attended a mass celebrated by a priest in favour of union with Rome.

The end came on 29th May when Mohammed II, grown weary of the long siege, decided to finish the battle with one violent overwhelming assault. The population of Constantinople learned of the sultan's decision and passed the night in prayer. In the church of St Sofia a solemn ceremony was held, the last ever Christian ceremony to be celebrated in the cathedral.

Promise of loot

The sultan had promised his troops a certain prize in the event of victory— three days of sacking and looting.

Attracted by the mirage of fabulous treasures in Constantinople the Turkish troops redoubled their efforts, but the first two waves of attackers were repulsed. The streets of the city were now deserted; every fit man was fighting on the walls. People unable to fight had taken refuge in the churches and were praying. Religious rivalries were at last forgotten.

But Giovanni Giustiniani was badly wounded and had to retire from the battle. This was an irreparable loss. The ensuing battle was bitterly fought and for 22 hours the outcome remained in doubt. Then suddenly a unit of Turkish

into pieces. Thousands of citizens died by the sword. Thousands of others were taken to the Turkish ships to be sold into slavery.

The fall of Constantinople had grave consequences. Turkish power continued to spread westwards. Venice had to fight against them on her own territory. In 1480 the Turks landed in Otranto, in 1517 they took Egypt, in 1522 Rhodes, and in 1527 they destroyed a Hungarian army at Mohacs on the Danube.

These victories induced Francis I of France to begin to think seriously of an alliance with Turkey. Eventually that alliance came about, and thanks to it the Turkish empire entered the field of European politics.

soldiers discovered a small unguarded gate near the Gate of Adrianople.

This may have been the result of treachery by one of the defenders. The little gate, known as the Circus Gate, opened into a ditch that led directly into the city; the defenders on the walls, who had by then repulsed a third attack, suddenly saw Turkish soldiers behind them.

The shouts of the exultant Turks drowned the sound of the prayers and hymns in the temple of St Sofia. Fighting was still continuing on the battlements. Among the defenders was Constantine himself who had been fighting courageously since the first onslaught. He was killed soon afterwards, his body recognized by the purple trimmings on his garments.

The massacre

The following day Mohammed II held a service of thanksgiving for the victory in the temple of St Sofia but this time the service was held according to the rites of Islam.

It is impossible to describe the violence of the massacre that followed the victory. Precious materials were torn up, pictures, statues and mosaics broken

A light cavalryman in the Turkish army.

A statuette of Catherine Segurana, the washer-woman heroine of the siege of Nice. She is depicted snatching the flag from a Turkish standard bearer.

CHAPTER 6

THE SIEGE OF NICE

In the first half of the 16th century France and Spain were already strong kingdoms, Francis I ruling in France and Charles V in Spain. With their countries now politically stabilized, their rulers could afford to look around and take note of what was happening outside their borders. This included watching for an opportunity to extend their dominions at the expense of their neighbours.

At that time it was still taken for granted that sovereignty over a country depended not only on the will of the people but on heredity and marriage. Royal marriages were therefore arranged. Towards the end of the 17th century, William of Orange became William III of Britain by his marriage to a princess, Mary, who became queen.

Power through marriage

Sovereignty by heredity or through marriage was a working principle that often caused serious clashes between countries, even as late as the 18th and 19th centuries, and the resulting military clashes were often disastrous for the countries over which the armies fought.

Thus in the first half of the 16th century Italy paid a heavy price for being an object of rivalry between France and Spain which were contending for the dominion of Europe and of the Italian peninsula in particular.

At that time, Italy was still a long way from being either united or independent. It was a collection of many small states and small powers and, being disunited, was an easy prey for any great power able to command a large army.

France and Spain were such countries, and they came into conflict over their claims to the kingdom of Naples. France claimed this in the name of the House of Anjou, which had been dispossessed of Naples by the Spaniards of the House of Aragon. Spain, already master of Sicily, immediately supported the counter claims of Aragon.

A similar situation arose in the case of the Duchy of Milan, where the French wanted to replace the Spanish-supported Sforza family with the house of Orleans.

Strategic position

The Duchy of Savoy, lying between France and the Duchy of Milan, held a strategic position. It dominated the alpine passes through which any French army would have to march to reach Italy. An alliance with Savoy would, therefore, be of great military value to either contender.

Duke Charles III, Duke of Savoy, was the uncle of Francis I of France and brother-in-law of Charles V of Spain. He was in no position, militarily, to oppose either.

In 1531, Charles V, now wearing the crown of the Holy Roman Empire and therefore ruler of Austria and Germany as well as Spain, gave to Charles III the country of Asti and the dominions of Charasco and Ceva. Francis I, although he had no right to these lands, opposed his uncle in this and made claims on the province of Nice. Because of its geographical strategic position and the strength of its castle, Nice constituted an obstacle on the way out of Italy.

The Pope mediates

Hilt of the sword belonging to the Holy Roman Emperor, Charles V.

When Pope Clement VII, wishing to make peace between Francis I and Charles V, asked the king of France for a meeting, Francis agreed. He insisted, however, on the meeting taking place at Nice and then only after it had been handed over by the Duke of Savoy to the Pope for the duration of their talks. Duke Charles, suspecting a trap, refused.

Nevertheless the meeting between Francis and the Pope took place but at Marseilles in 1533, on the occasion of the marriage of Catherine Medici to Henry, second son of Francis I.

Here was yet another political match, and this one resulted in the Pope's transferring his support from the Spanish Habsburgs and the Empire to the French Valois.

Defection and treaty

French artillery at the time of King Francis I of France.

This was followed by a serious blow to Francis I. The great Genoese admiral Andrea Doria, then an ally of the French, defected and placed himself at the service of the Emperor. By this single stroke, Francis I lost his naval supremacy in the Mediterranean. He had, therefore, to find himself a new ally and this he found in Turkey with which he signed a treaty in 1536.

It was a complete treaty for defensive and offensive co-operation, a treaty moreover with a Moslem empire, and it horrified the Catholic world.

The ruler of Turkey at that time was the sultan Suleiman the Magnificent. The Turkish fleet was commanded by the famous corsair Khair-ed-din, known as Barbarossa, lord of Algiers. Khair-ed-din had already raided many of the coastal cities of southern Italy, inflicting severe damage on them.

On land, the whole Balkan peninsula was firmly in the hands of the Turks and they had many times threatened the very heart of the Habsburg power, even attacking Vienna and Hungary. They had been repulsed at great cost but it had been impossible to prevent their sacking many cities where they committed atrocious massacres. Many of the prisoners taken had been sold later as slaves in Turkish markets.

Unholy alliance

The whole of Europe was therefore now drawn up against the Turks, so the news that France had formed an alliance with them came like a thunderbolt. The "Unholy Alliance" made by

France had been virtually in force since 25th February, 1525, when Francis himself had been taken prisoner by the Turks at the battle of Pavia. His mother, Luisa of Savoy, in agreement with her chancellor, Duprat, began negotiations with the Turks for his release. The agreements reached then were brought forward and included in the 1536 treaty.

This alliance caused great bloodshed in Europe and led to the atrocities committed during the siege of Nice. The exact clauses of the 1536 treaty are not known and have never been revealed, but as far back as 1534, Francis I envisaged naval attacks by Barbarossa against Naples, Sicily, Sardinia and Spain, while the French army was to attack on land.

Pretext for war

In November 1535, Francesco Sforza II died at Milan. Spain took possession of the Duchy and this gave the king of France a pretext for the resumption of hostilities. He attacked the Duchy of Savoy and within a few days only Nice and Vercelli were left to Duke Charles. With his seven-year-old son, Emmanuel Philibert, the duke took up residence in the castle of Nice which dominated the city and the sea, and it was there

that his wife, the Duchess, died.

Charles V of Spain decided to reply to the French provocation by invading Provence. He crossed the French border in 1536 but achieved no positive results. The French evaded battle and sealed themselves off in the trenches of Avignon after having destroyed every possible source of supply.

The Imperial troops found themselves advancing through a desert and were eventually decimated by hunger and disease. They were forced to with-

French dress of the mid-16th century. In the foreground are nobles and lords, behind are common people and merchants.

Nice at the time of the siege in 1543.

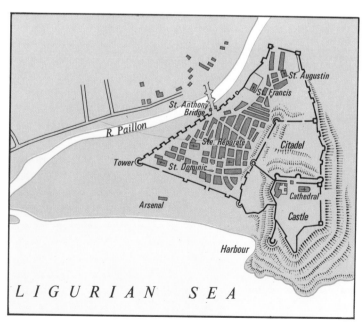

Two corsairs from the Barbary Coast who were present at the siege of Nice. One of them was accused of practising black magic: he succeeded in hitting his targets by using his crossbow as a sextant.

draw. But the French were now also in difficulties and so were unable to make any move against Duke Charles.

Truce

The desire for peace was now so strongly felt on both sides that a truce had to be arranged. A meeting between Charles V and Francis I was suggested, and a request was made that the new Pope Paul III should also be present. The meeting place suggested was the castle of Nice.

Charles V was now so weak in the military sense that everyone was sure the plan would succeed. On 9th May, 1538, he disembarked at Villafranca (Villefranche), a few miles from Nice. Paul III was already on his way there from Rome. Francis I had not yet consented to the meeting but it appears that everyone thought he had done so some time earlier.

Then suddenly Duke Charles and the people of Nice refused permission for the conference to take place in the castle. They did not even want Paul III to lodge there, although he had expressly requested it. There were rumours of treachery and plots. According to these, the Pope and the Emperor were going to kidnap Emmanuel Philibert and then occupy the castle by force.

The people took up arms and began to organize the castle's defences. The Emperor, shocked by their obstinacy, remained on his flagship, the *Andrea Doria*. When the Pope arrived at Nice,

Stone cannon balls fired at the city from the Turkish galleys, now in the Massena Museum in Nice.

he took up residence in a monastery after hearing Duke Charles's explanation and a meeting was arranged to take place at Monaco the neighbouring principality.

Uneasy peace

Francis I was not present but he sent delegates and on 18th June, 1538, the truce was signed. The agreement was that it would last for at least ten years. It was, in fact, to last for only four, and that precariously.

Finally in July, 1538, Francis I and Charles V met at Aigues-Mortes and peace seemed assured because of the friendliness of the meeting which lasted for several days.

But the friendliness was an illusion. Suleiman and his Turks attacked Hungary again and captured what is now Budapest. Charles V, in an attempt to lessen Turkish pressure on Europe, launched a naval attack against Algeria where he narrowly missed losing his life during a storm following Barbarossa's counter-attack.

Turkish support

Francis I, for his part, continued a diplomatic offensive with the aim of securing Turkish military support at the decisive moment. At the beginning of July, 1541, his ambassador to Constantinople, Antoine Rincon, was murdered by imperial soldiers near Pavia, in territory belonging to the Duchy of Milan.

This crime furnished Francis with the right to insist that the sultan should invade the Duchy. But Suleiman hesitated for two years before making his decision to intervene in support of Francis.

Suleiman addressed a letter to the king of France, saying that he had ordered Barbarossa to put to sea and place himself at the disposal of the French king and of Rincon's successor,

Plan of the port of Villafranca, from a 17th century print. The star-shaped Boron fort, built after the siege, can be seen in the upper left-hand corner. Barbarossa placed his artillery on this site during the siege.

Below, the Boron fort as it appears today.

The Bay at Villafranca. It was here that Barbarossa's Turkish galleys dropped anchor.

Antoine Paulin. Paulin, self-styled Baron de la Garde, was a mysterious figure and an adventurer, about whom history has little to say.

Khair-ed-din set sail for Marseilles with 110 galleys and 14,000 men, and there joined up with a French fleet of 40 galleys and 7,000 men under Paulin's command.

The arrival of a great Turkish naval and military force came as no surprise to the inhabitants of Nice. Rumours of a possible French attack on the city had been circulating in the spring of 1543 when Charles V, on his way from Spain to Germany, was passing through Busseto en route for his meeting with Pope Paul III.

75

The attack begins

The attack on Nice began on 16th June, launched by sixteen galleys under the command of Count Louis de Grignan, lieutenant general of Provence. He was helped by a traitor from Nice, Benedetti Grimaldi.

Four galleys tried to disembark at Lympia but came under attack from the defending guns and were driven off, later to be captured at sea and taken to Genoa. Magdalon, their captain, was gravely wounded during the engagement, but before he died he disclosed the fact that the Turkish fleet would soon be arriving in Provence.

As a result, when Khair-ed-din's 110 galleys sailed past Nice on 5th July, 1543, heading for Marseilles, the Duke of Savoy and the men of Nice were not taken by surprise.

It is possible that at this point Francis I had some misgivings. Perhaps he realized that what he was about to do was cruel and wicked. But Khair-ed-din would give him no time for reflection. He had not sailed out with a whole fleet purely as a threatening gesture. Each day of inactivity cost money and affected the morale of his crews, and Khair-ed-din pressed Paulin to force the king to give the order to attack Nice. In the end, Francis ordered the attack.

A coin minted in Nice during the siege; on one side is the coat of arms of Savoy, on the reverse side, in Latin, can be seen the abbreviated words, "Nice besieged by the Turks and French 1543".

A happy city

Up to then, Nice had been a happy place and a vivid portrait of the city in 1547 has been left by a courtier, Gerolamo Nunzio, who lived from 1496 to 1576 and who was a member of Emmanuel Philibert's entourage. After talking about the surroundings of Nice and its valley—"well cultivated and pleasant and adorned with gardens full of lemon and orange trees"— Nunzio gives this description of its inhabitants:—"they are all industrious and all engaged in trade and commerce;... and the men from here make some of the best sailors along this whole coast. The city is very thickly populated and could provide up to three or four thousand good soldiers.

"There are gentlemen and lords, with estates and castles; but they live, not in the city but in their own places, particularly when the court is not in Nice. They are not very well-educated, and they come from the mountains; they are not very friendly towards out-

This painting of the defence of Nice by the Italian writer, politician and painter Massimo d'Azeglio, is in the Gallery of Modern Art in Turin.

siders. Among themselves they have the best time in the world: they dance every day and have parties in the streets.

"But the social classes do not mix, so that the parties are held in several places. In one there are the nobles, in another the merchants. Here there are artisans and there there are labourers; and the unmarried girls are the ones who keep the parties going. They come out covered with flowers and greenery; they are bareheaded or they wear hats. There is not one who has not got posies of flowers hanging around her ears, and in her hair, and here, and there, and on her head, so that six and seven bunches of flowers are usually to be seen decorating the head of each one of them. Then they have flowers at their bosoms and flowers in their hands. And they are so bedecked with flowers that every time you meet one of them it is like seeing another Flora."

The Day of War

But the fury of war, the result of Francis I's excessive ambition, was soon to fall upon all this gaiety and fun.

There were six companies of arquebusiers posted throughout the city. The city walls, which were not very strong, had only three hundred soldiers to guard what Nunzio had described as "a valley well-cultivated and adorned with gardens". The defence of the built-up part of the city and its walls was entrusted to a brave man, Andrea Odinet, Count of Montfort. The men guarding the castle awaited the arrival of Paolo Simeoni de' Baldi, Knight of St John of Malta, and a veteran of the wars against the Mohammedans.

The people of Nice were now threatened with assault by Barbarossa's naval force of 14,000 men, Paulin's French fleet with 7,000 men and, from 11th August, another 12,000 Frenchmen under the command of Francis de Bourbon-Vendôme. In addition to this, a company of Tuscans and a band of volunteers from Provence, in the service of Paulin, had also marched on Nice.

Among the traitors from Nice who had gone over to serve France, there was another Grimaldi—Jean-Baptiste de Beuil, a most bitter enemy of the house of Savoy. Popular opinion considered him responsible for a number of crimes, including an attempt to poison Emmanuel Philibert.

Marble bust of Catherine Sagurana which formerly stood on the Paieroliera Gate and is now in the Massena Museum in Nice.

Barbarossa

While the French army was marching on Nice, Barbarossa was also on the move. On 5th August, he entered Villafranca, a town separated from Nice by the promontory of Montboron, and had begun to prepare gun emplacements for artillery of varying calibres. He had, in all, seventy-five cannon.

Two envoys from Nice tried to have talks with the corsair, but they were received instead by Paulin. Paulin treated them to a meal and, chatting courteously, tried to convince them that Nice would be safer under a powerful lord like the king of France than under a poor, weak one like Duke Charles III. The envoys deeply offended, refused every offer of a treaty.

The following day, 6th August, one of Paulin's heralds took the first offer of surrender to Nice. Montfort replied that he would hold on at all costs.

Heavy fighting

On 7th August, the Turks disembarked in force and made a violent assault on the city. An hour's heavy fighting followed.

Taking advantage of the confusion, Paolo Simeoni de' Baldi, with about fifty determined men, succeeded in entering the city and the castle, where his arrival was anxiously awaited. The Turks were repulsed and the defenders began to realize that they now had some chance of holding out.

On 10th August, a new order to surrender came from Paulin. On the 11th, a Saturday, the troops of Count d'Enghien entered the field. The Count ordered Jean-Baptiste Grimaldi to draw up another ultimatum. This was entrusted to a French drummer and to Benedetti Grimaldi, the man who had headed the attack on 16th June.

Turkish envoys

Grimaldi presented himself at one of the gates to the citizens of Nice, certain that he would be welcomed as a saviour. Instead he was arrested and subjected to three hours of flogging in the castle. He was then strangled and hung up by one foot from the wall for the enemy to see. The drummer, on the other hand, was given the respect required by the laws of war and returned to his own side with another refusal from Nice.

On the 12th, 13th and 14th of August, bombardments and assaults followed close upon each other. On the 14th a nephew of Khair-ed-din's was killed by a shot fired from the castle. To avenge him, Barbarossa beheaded Giovanni Boyer, a prisoner captured on 7th August.

At dawn on 15th August, 120 galleys sailed out of the bay of Villafranca, rounded the promontory of Montboron and hove to before the city. At 8 a.m. all their guns began to fire a tremendous cannonade.

Infiltration

The bombardment opened a breach in the walls near the Paieroliera gate which guarded the city to the north and which was also called St Sebastian's gate. Turks and Frenchmen hurled themselves at it in a great rush, armed with ladders to scale the walls—but the defence did not weaken.

Resistance was also desperate at the pentagonal tower, known as the Sincaire tower, against which Barbarossa threw his own personal guard of janissaries. Supporting them were Tuscan soldiers and the men of Paulin's Provençal division.

Suddenly a Turkish ensign succeeded in reaching the top of the breach. There he planted the red Saracen flag with its crescent symbol. But on the battlements of Nice was a washer-woman who, with other women, had stood since dawn by the side of the defenders. Armed only with a small shovel, the mark of her occupation—she hurled herself at the Turk and tore the flag

This 19th century print shows the men of Nice on the walls of the Sincaire bastion at a crucial moment in the battle. Catherine Sagurana can be seen with the commandant, the daring Andrea Odinet, Count of Montfort.

out of his hand. At her cry of victory, the men of Nice took heart and chased the enemy from the breach.

This woman was called Catherine Sagurana, known in the city by the nickname "badly made". Her exploit probably belongs to the realm of legend and many people believe that there are more elements of fantasy in the episode than historical fact. Whatever the truth, it was a heroic day for the people of Nice. They became more resolute and fought with renewed vigour and a new fervour.

Rape of a countryside

When the Turks and the French were driven back they left 300 dead and wounded on the field. They returned to their starting line and their artillery alone continued the battle. That day no fewer than 965 cannon shots were fired against Nice.

During the following days, the Turkish infantry ran riot in the countryside, sacking and destroying, while the artillery continued its bombardment of the city. The walls gave way in several places and Montfort realized that to continue defending the city would mean condemning it to destruction.

He therefore sent out a peace offer to d'Enghien on 23rd August.

The city entered

The first French entered the city along with Strozzi's Tuscans and Paulin's Provençal division, commanded by Jean-Baptiste Grimaldi. Barbarossa was begged not to allow his Turks to enter. He agreed unwillingly and sent them back to Villafranca.

On 24th August, the Duke d'Enghien sent a message to the castle defenders. In it he informed them that they could leave the castle if they wished before the bombardment recommenced. About 500 people, many of them women and children, accepted the invitation and left the fortress and the city.

On 28th August the battle for the castle was renewed and continued until 2nd September, with bombardments, sorties, mining and countermining. On 5th September d'Enghien sent a drummer and once again demanded surrender. The reply was such that there could be no further exchanges or messages for the remainder of the siege.

The French suddenly found them-

The ruins of the Castle of Nice seen from opposite sides. The castle was built on the site of a religious building.

selves without ammunition and had to borrow from the Turks. Barbarossa, already angered because his force had not been allowed to sack the city, amused himself by teasing Paulin. He pointed out that, while at Marseilles, the French had nothing better to do than fill barrels with wine instead of gunpowder. The great Moslem admiral even threatened to abandon his allies altogether and set sail for Rome. But in the end he gave up the idea and yielded to the insistences of d'Enghien.

Meanwhile, news had arrived that an imperial army was only two days' march from Nice, and to add to their problems it now began to rain heavily. Disconcerted, the Turks and the French abandoned their positions on land and retreated in disorder to the boats.

Then on 7th September, the artillery was recalled. On 8th September, the Turks came ashore and began to loot the city. Barbarossa sent back to the sultan four shiploads of booty, worth about six hundred ducats, as well as 2,500 slaves. But they did not reach Suleiman. The ships were intercepted by the Aragonese at Naples and taken back to Nice. Meanwhile, the French, having nothing better to do, set fire to the city and then withdrew beyond the river Varo which marked the frontier with France.

The Turkish fleet set sail for Toulon while seven groups of imperial soldiers entered Nice. A few days later the imperial fleet, under the command of Giannetino Doria, took Duke Charles III and the governor of Milan to Villafranca where they disembarked on 13th September during a violent thunderstorm.

Nice had known pestilence and famine during the war between Francis I and Charles V. It was to know pestilence again in 1550 and 1580, and changed hands several times before becoming the fine French city that everyone knows today. In 1600, it was taken by the Duke de Guise. In 1686, it was restored to Savoy but its citadel and ramparts were destroyed by French attack in 1706. It was given back to Savoy by the Treaty of Utrecht in 1713. It was after this treaty that the new town was built. In 1792, it was taken by the armies of the French Republic and remained French until 1814, when it reverted again to Sardinia. It was finally ceded to France in 1860 by a treaty between the King of Sardinia and Napoleon III.

CHAPTER 7

VIENNA

Situated at the confluence of the Danube and the Wien rivers the geographical location of Vienna made it important both economically and strategically in all the wars between East and West, that is between the Romano-German and the Slav-Hungarian worlds. Its commercial and strategic importance did not escape the Romans, and during the reign of the Emperor Augustus it was a base for Roman flotillas operating on the Danube.

At that time it was called Vindobona. Later, when the municipality spread, it took its present German name from the River Wien which flows through the centre of modern Vienna in the part known as the Innere Stadt.

Barbarians attack

With the decline of the Roman Empire, began the assault by barbarians from the north. During such forays and invasions Vienna was always a principal objective. Marcus Aurelius died there in A.D. 180 during a campaign against the rebel Marcomanni and Quadi tribes.

Some years earlier these tribes had reached as far as northern Italy but were eventually driven out. Attila carried out a raid in the 5th century. Tradition relates that in the 8th century the city was attacked by the forces of Charlemagne. Later it was fought over by Germans and Magyars. In the year 881 it was called Venia for the first time.

By 1137, it had become a main town of the border area and a hereditary duchy. Throughout the centuries it became increasingly important as a military stronghold and a Christian bulwark against the forces of the East. It withstood attacks by Slavs, Magyars and Turks and repelled them.

Turkish invasion

In 1529 a Turkish army under the command of Suleiman the Magnificent marched on Vienna. This army had come fresh from its triumph at the battle of Mohacs, and had invaded Hungary in force to put down a rebellion and place on the throne a puppet king, John Szapolyai. The legitimate king of Hungary and Bohemia was Ferdinand I, Archduke of Austria and future Holy Roman Emperor. The Turkish armies overthrew Ferdinand's Budapest outposts, after which Vienna lay open to them.

In reply to this threat a combined German-Spanish army marched to the defence of the city. It was sent by the Emperor Charles V who had renounced his hereditary possessions in Austria in favour of Ferdinand I. This German-Spanish force, twenty thousand strong, garrisoned Vienna from 26th September to 16th October, 1529, and succeeded in holding off the Turkish army. They were helped in this by the bad weather conditions which prevented the Turks from moving their siege artillery into position.

John Sobieski, king of Poland, arrives at Vienna leading his winged hussars at a crucial moment in the decisive battle of Kahlenberg.

Ich will sie zer schlagen, ünd sie for

A spectacular scene towards the end of the battle for Vienna before the raising of the siege.

kennen sie sollen mier unter meine Füsse fallen soll itzliegn:

Rout of the Turks

The Turkish retreat turned into a disastrous rout. Suleiman's army, falling back on Adrianople, was harried by pursuing cavalry and trapped by the blizzards of an early winter. Despite the disastrous retreat the sultan of Turkey refused to negotiate peace until 1533, and even then he gave up fighting only on land. At sea he carried on the war against Charles V.

Vienna saved

Vienna had survived a severe threat and was conscious of the narrowness of its escape. With the defeat of the Turks, work began on strengthening the city's fortifications. The Tuscan engineers, Pierpaolo Floriani, Giovanni Pieroni and Alessandro del Borro, worked on them in 1610.

On 7th October, 1571, the Turks were defeated at Lepanto. This was a straight battle between Christian and Turkish forces and the greater part of the Turkish fleet was destroyed.

Historically this battle is important in two ways. It was the last battle in which oar-propelled vessels were used on both sides, and its casualties were very high for the period. The Christian forces lost 8,000 men killed and double that number wounded. Twenty-five thousand Turks died but the number wounded was never known. After the battle, 15,000 Christians were released from slavery in Turkish galleys.

This battle put an end to the Turks' offensive in the central and western Mediterranean and forced them into a period of quiet. They did not take up the offensive again until 1645, when they began by attacking the Hungarian border and the Venetian-owned fortress of Candia in Crete. Candia held out under siege until 1669. Hungary was then still part of the Ottoman empire, as laid down in the treaty following the battle of Mohacs.

Sultan Mohammed IV, who reigned in Turkey from 1648 to 1687 and ordered the attack on Vienna in 1683.

New threats

The threat to Vienna came in 1663 when an army of 100,000 Turks invaded Hungary. The invasion was timed to coincide with the revolt of the Magyar nobility against the emperor, Leopold I.

It was a disastrous moment for Vienna which would almost certainly have fallen had not the Imperial Army defeated the Turks at St Gothard on the River Rába. It was a decisive victory and the Turks retreated over the border. By the Treaty of Vasvár they agreed to a twenty-year truce.

In the meantime, the bloody Thirty Years' War was in progress in northern Europe. The Holy Roman Empire, as Voltaire was to say, was no longer Holy or Roman or an Empire. It was disintegrating.

In the north, the Swedes were growing powerful. In France the star of Louis XIV was rising. The "Sun King" was then at the height of his aggressive expansionist policy and was in process of annexing Strasbourg and Casale, both of which were valuable stepping stones to further expansion in Germany and Italy. Thus Europe was in a serious state of imbalance and this was not long in provoking new conflicts.

And new conflicts

Meanwhile trouble was boiling up again on the Danube. In 1678 the restive Hungarians had risen yet again against the Empire and had made an alliance with the Turks. The treaty of Vasvár was broken.

Once again the Turks invaded Habsburg Hungary and in March 1683 they marched on Vienna.

The Turkish army with its rich baggage trains moved northwards from their assembly at Adrianople. The faint-hearted sultan, Mohammed IV, with all his court and his harem in more than 100 carriages, followed the army only as far as Belgrade.

There it was joined by contingents from other parts of the Turkish Empire —spahis and janissaries (soldiers of the standing Turkish army, often Christian boys captured as slaves and trained as soldiers), Bosnian Turks, Slavs and Tartars.

The Turkish army totalled about 100,000 men and was led by the ambitious Grand Vizier Kara Mustafa. The army's orders were "Vienna, Prague and then the Rhine and the Tiber".

Europe off balance

Europe was quite unprepared for this threat. There was no common defence policy. On the contrary, Louis XIV's diplomats did their utmost to support the Turks against Austria. When Emperor Leopold asked for allies, only a few heads of state declared their support for him.

The Pope offered money, as did Spain, Portugal and the Italian states. King John Sobieski of Poland promised Austria military aid. So did the German principalities of Bavaria, Saxony and Franconia. But many others, the most important being the Grand Elector of Brandenburg, held aloof from the war.

Disunited front

If all these offers of help had been co-ordinated and immediately forthcoming, they would have added up to an army of about 80,000 men, but there was neither time nor co-ordination. So the commander-designate, Duke Charles V of Lorraine, was faced with an impossible task—that of accepting battle with 24,000 men against an army of 100,000.

Realizing that he had no chance in the open field, he decided to lead his army to the shelter of the fortifications of Vienna and to hold out there until help arrived from the north and west.

When the Turkish vanguard reached the Wienerwald (the famous Vienna

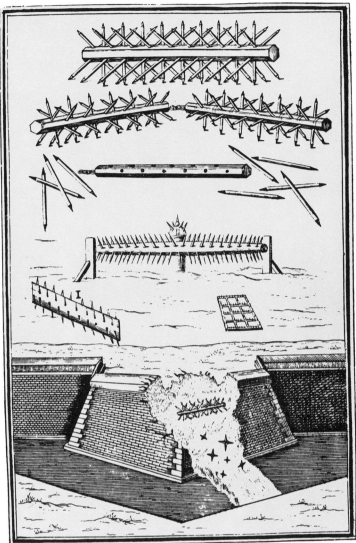

Illustrations from a famous treatise on military art (Les Travaux De Mars, ou L'Art De La Guerre by Alain Manesson Mallet 1696). Shown here are "Friesian Horses" and other obstacles used as barricades at points liable to surprise attack by enemy infantry. Also illustrated, a sapper of the time equipped for attacking fortifications.

woods immortalized by Strauss) on 7th July, 1683, the emperor Leopold I and his court fled from the city. Charles of Lorraine appointed Count Ernst Rüdiger von Starhemberg to take charge of the defending infantry while he took up position in open country with his cavalry.

The destiny of Europe

Meanwhile, the Turkish army entered the woods and occupied them. Around the city, the first fires were lit and soon the first raids were made. This was an anxious time of waiting for Europe as well as Vienna—for the destiny of Vienna and Austria was the destiny of Europe itself.

Even in those days Vienna was a gay city but the gay, carefree citizens resolutely united to face the threat from without. The impressive defence works were feverishly strengthened, an example being set by the courageous and tireless Burgermeister Liebenberg. Count Starhemberg assumed supreme command of the fortress, for the defence of which he could count on only 16,000 men, including citizen volunteers. University students banded together under the direction of their rector. Corporations of artisans formed volunteer companies. Other groups, composed of women, set themselves to digging trenches.

Above, a Turkish musket. Below, a lead rod used by infantry to make shot when the supply of ammunition became exhausted.

The siege begins

On 14th July, the main force of the Turkish army appeared in front of the city and prepared for the siege which was to last two months. An immense encampment was built in a semi-circle and the attacks began. The most violent were concentrated at the Burg and Schotten gates, élite formations of janissaries and other Turkish troops being used. Their Balkan allies lined up on the north-west near Heiligenstadt.

On the same day Charles of Lorraine crossed the Danube with his small cavalry force and destroyed the bridge behind them. Then the Turks crossed the branch of the river called the Donaukanal and shut off the city from the north.

From the first day of the siege, the grand vizier knew that the city could not be taken by a single attack. It would, therefore, be necessary to proceed by stages, using the usual methods of mining and blockade. Vienna would have to fall through starvation.

Disease and bombardment

Dysentery and all kinds of illnesses, apart from the food shortage, quickly weakened the besieged Viennese. Many workers were ready to give up and were rallied only by speeches, offers of good wages and finally by coercion.

An almost uninterrupted bombardment fell upon the defences and houses. Fires broke out all over the city. Mines set under the walls and ramparts by a corps of French engineers gradually demolished the fortifications, and all the time attacks were being launched by the investing forces.

The defenders' strength was sapped daily. On the night of 6th September, a messenger swam across the Danube carrying an appeal for help from Starhemberg to Lorraine. The gist of this was that there was no time to be lost. Lorraine did not hesitate. That very day he moved to the passage over the Danube with his army of liberation. This numbered 27,000 Austrians and 15,000 Poles under John Sobieski, as well as Saxons, Bavarians, Swedes and Franks. His total force was 65,000 men.

Reinforcements

On the 9th of September, Lorraine was advancing through the Wienerwald. Rockets were fired to announce to the garrison that help was at hand. They replied with joyous shouts from the

ramparts of Mölker. On 11th September, before the incredulous eyes of Kara Mustafa, the combined troops were deployed in the Wienerwald.

According to the records of the time, the night of 11/12th September was warm and soft. At 4 a.m. on the 12th a Capuchin monk, the papal legate, celebrated mass at an altar which was erected on drums placed side by side in the sacristy of the church at Kahlenberg. At sunrise, the army prepared itself for battle.

Kara Mustafa, despite advice from his second-in-command, Ibrahim, to raise the siege when the army of liberation appeared, now saw himself obliged to fight from an unfavourable position on all fronts. John Sobieski lined up his army on the right, the German troops took up the centre position, and the Austrians the left.

The siege is lifted

John Sobieski successfully attacked the body of the Turkish army. His legendary hussars found themselves surrounded but, backed up by the German infantry, they broke the circle and won a splendid victory. The siege was raised. Italian cuirassiers stopped and dispersed the best of the Turkish cavalry as they were making a last desperate attack. All was over at 5 o'clock in the afternoon and Vienna welcomed her liberators.

Kara Mustafa sought refuge at Belgrade where he was executed shortly afterwards by order of the sultan.

Among the messages of congratulations that arrived at the Habsburg court was one, sent for reasons of etiquette, from King Louis. The French king used the word "miracle" in referring to the unexpected liberation of Vienna.

Another picture of the battle for Vienna, from a painting by F. Gaffels. Note the Turkish trenches before the city. These were used for protection during the approach to the walls.

CHAPTER 8

TURIN

The War of the Spanish Succession was waged between France, Spain and Bavaria on the one side, and Britain, Holland, Austria, Prussia, Hanover, Portugal, the Duchy of Savoy and the German States of the Roman Empire on the other. The struggle raged in Spain, in Italy, in Germany, in the Low Countries, on the ocean and in the North Sea.

The war was fought over the succession to the throne of Spain, and to understand why it came about it is necessary to understand the events leading up to it.

France and Spain had fought a bloody war in the 16th century which had come to an end with the signing of the Treaty of Câteau-Cambrésis on 3rd April, 1559. The siege of Nice had been one of the most famous episodes in this war. This peace confirmed Spanish domination in Europe which lasted for a long time in Italy but was short-lived elsewhere.

Spain dominates

For more than a century and a half Spain controlled southern Italy and the islands. She also controlled the Duchy of Milan. The rest of the Italian peninsula was a mosaic of little states, each with its own master.

At the time of the war between France and Spain the Spanish king was Charles I. He was also Charles V of the Roman Empire, and thus ruled Austria and

Germany as well as Spain. In 1556 the Habsburgs split into two branches, one of which was to continue to govern Austria and the Roman Empire of the German States, the other to rule Spain.

This second branch, the Spanish branch, died out in 1700 when the last Spanish Habsburg, Charles II, died leaving no direct heir. But although he left no direct heir there were many claimants among those who could show any kind of relationship with the ruling house of Spain. Furthermore, in these days any relationship with the monarchy meant power, and royal marriages were of political importance.

Among the claimants to the Spanish throne were Leopold I, Emperor of Austria, Louis XIV, King of France, and Victor Amadeus II, Duke of Savoy.

Casus belli

A few weeks before his death, Charles II had named a grandson of Louis XIV as his successor. This was Philip of Anjou. That was sufficient to stir to action the contending parties in Europe and to unleash the first great war of the modern age.

Victor Amadeus did not enter the war at once. He waited until 1703 when he joined the anti-French league after seeing Louis XIV's armies defeated at Carpi near Verona, at Chiari near Bressa and at Cremona between 1701 and 1702. The commander of the forces which had defeated the French in these

A large wall musket used at the siege of Turin 1706.

A detail from a large painting by an unknown artist showing a decisive moment in the battle for Turin. The painting is now in the Risorgimento Museum in Rome.

battles was Eugene of Savoy, second cousin of Victor. Victor now thought that he could safely take possession of the Milanese territory he had so long dreamed of annexing to Piedmont.

The armies march

Unfortunately, Victor did not choose his moment well. Eugene had had to return to Vienna and Victor found himself forced to face the French army on his own. Between 1704 and 1706 the French invaded Piedmont and left only several fortresses and the capital, Turin, in Victor's hands.

On 14th May, 1706, 44,000 Franco-Spanish troops, under the command of Louis d'Aubusson, Duc de la Feuillade, laid siege to the Piedmontese capital. Victor, however, managed to leave the city with a picked cavalry unit and scoured the countryside searching for Eugene whose assistance was now required at Turin.

Defending Turin was a large army mainly of Piedmontese troops plus six imperial battalions. The commander in charge was the Austrian, Philipp Lorenz, Count von Daun, at that time 38 years old. Von Daun was destined for a brilliant career. He was a man of great energy despite the fact that he had been crippled by a leg wound.

Gunpowder and the new style war

A French cavalryman returns to camp after a foraging expedition.

Turin was then a far less sprawling city than it is today. It was protected on the north by the river Doria and on the east by the river Po. Its western and southern walls had been strengthened by new fortifications of the rampart type and by great wedge-like projections of masonry. It was at the siege of Turin that mine warfare began to mean what it means in the modern sense—mining quite different from that seen at Alesia and during the Crusades.

The invention of gunpowder and its

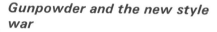

adoption for military use had given great impetus to the art of mining. By the old method holes from which attacks were made, were dug under the walls. The new method was by blowing up the walls by means of gunpowder planted beneath them. Naturally the enemy replied to this with countermining just as in ancient times.

A great feat of mining in the modern style took place in 1669 at the siege of

Candia (modern Heraklion), capital of the island of Crete. The Venetians besieged in Candia set off 610 mines and killed 1,200 of the investing Turks. Mining on this scale was used at the siege of Turin in 1706 especially in the area under the Citadel.

King's engineer

Another fact must be noted if we are to understand the nature of the siege of Turin. Next in rank to the Duc de la Feuillade was Sebastien le Prestre, Marquis de Vauban, one of the most famous military engineers of all time. He was born in St. Léger near Avallon in 1633 and by the time of the siege was a man of wide experience and highly honoured.

At the age of twenty-two he had been named "the King's Engineer" by

Another incident in the battle for Turin, from a painting by J. Merchtenburg.

Cardinal Mazarin. Vauban had constructed and modernized 160 French fortresses; he had taken part in 140 battles and directed fifty sieges. He had also evolved the following theory for capturing a fortified city.

The operation was to begin with a cavalry action which was intended to clear the surrounding countryside, disrupt communications and block all access roads. Infantry then encamped in the neighbourhood and began work on the inner and outer walls of fortifications, that is, the concentric circles we have already seen in use in Caesar's time. These rings were designed to protect the besieger from attacks by the besieged in front and from attacks by an army of reinforcements from the rear.

The five stages of attack

After the construction of the fortified circles, the attack followed five stages. The first consisted of digging a trench in front of the inner ring of fortifications and about 600 yards from the enemy. Here were sited the longest-range cannon.

Trenches were then dug forward in a zig-zag pattern. Next a new trench system was prepared, running parallel with the first one but this second trench line was 350 yards from the enemy front. In it other cannon were placed along with mortars which held the enemy fire while the infantry and labourers worked on the third stage of the approach pattern.

This third stage was a repetition of the

One of the underground tunnels of Turin. These tunnels, immediately below the citadel, were of great value in the defence during the siege.

second. Zig-zag saps were sent out from the second position to within 150 yards of the enemy and here a third trench system was dug parallel to the first two. It was from this third position that mines were operated. The trenches linking the three circles now acted as communication trenches.

The final stages

Now comes the fourth stage of Vauban's plan. When batteries from the first two trench systems blasted the opposition defences, infantry attacked from the third position to break in through any openings created by artillery or mines. This was the decisive moment.

The last stage was the destruction of the ramparts but this was only rarely achieved. The customs of the century laid down that at this point surrender was honourable and that fighting in a city containing civilians was senseless and cruel. Military etiquette even evolved a fixed procedure and moment for surrender.

According to some, a garrison could admit defeat and save its honour if, at the moment of surrender, less than half its defenders were still active in combat. More rigidly Vauban laid down that resistance must continue until two-thirds of the defenders were out of action.

Vauban's siege method was widely followed. It was used in Rome in 1849 and in the Crimea in 1856, but at Turin the Duc de la Feuillade wanted to carry out the siege in his own way. Vauban advised him to capture first of all the nearby Capuchin Hill, from which it was possible to look out over the whole city. The Duc preferred a direct frontal assault on the citadel, being certain of reaching a speedy victory in this way.

Storm of fire

He began by bombarding the city with a storm of cannon fire, using more than 800 cannonballs a day. The defenders covered the roofs of their houses with earth to soften the effects of the blows and lifted the paving stones from the roads to prevent them from being chipped.

After a first flutter of panic, when Victor Amadeus was seen leaving the

A relief model of Turin at the time of the siege. On the right can be seen the citadel and in the foreground the siege works of the French.

*Portrait of Pietro
Micca by V. Edel, in the
Military Museum in
Rome. The heroic soldier
is about to ignite the
powder that will blow
up the passageway and
block it against the
enemy. On the facing
page is the passage
way as it is today.*

capital in daylight, the Piedmontese recovered their spirits and made up their minds to resist. But they were plagued by desertions, for the French had let it be known that they would pay two gold louis to every soldier passing over to their lines.

There were spies at work too; a boy was caught while trying to take to the French lines an innocent looking pack of cards which in reality contained notes of the points where the French might usefully concentrate their artillery.

There was a severe shortage of gunpowder in the Piedmontese camp. Victor Amadeus, knowing this, had left orders that it should be used most sparingly. Count von Daun, after considering the situation carefully, decided to intensify his mine attacks against the besiegers, believing that this method would be more effective than using cannon and at the same time it would save gunpowder.

Subterranean war

Beneath Turin, spreading out into the country, there was an intricate maze of

subterranean tunnels and shafts. This enabled the Piedmontese, with only a few hundred mine-layers, to blow up parts of the French lines. One day in May they sank twenty-four French cannon by blowing up the ground underneath them. They also blew up three companies of grenadiers who were completely buried.

In the darkness of the tunnels the opposing troops searched for, found, and killed each other with a savagery intensified by fear. Whoever first lit the fuse saw his enemies die like rats in a trap. Then he had to hurry and find a way out himself before the gas from the explosion suffocated him.

Carbon monoxide lay heavily in the tunnels, asphyxiating soldiers two days after the explosion. The tunnels filled up with corpses and it was the task of condemned prisoners or boys from charity hospitals in the city to drag them out.

On 7th August the French forced an entry into one of the main tunnels and held it for some hours. This was a serious threat to the defenders for the attackers could at any moment have emerged at the rear of the defenders in the heart of the citadel. Luckily the attack did not develop. Count von Daun had already informed Victor by letter about this serious infiltration and warned him that the gunpowder in the city was by now almost used up. Victor replied, "Fight with your bayonets," and he urged them to continue the resistance as Eugene was now on the march with an army to relieve Turin.

French disagreements

On their side the French realized that every hour now counted. Philip, Duke of Orleans, a cousin of the king, arrived from Paris with 14,000 additional troops and, determined to capture Turin at any cost, took over the supreme command.

On 27th August the French exploded mines beneath the wall of the Mezzaluna del Soccorso and shortly after midnight a wave of French troops broke over the parapet and advanced rapidly. But at dawn they were driven back into the moat by a Piedmontese counter-attack and massacred by the artillery on the ramparts.

Towards evening the French asked for a truce and also for permission to go down into the moat and rescue the wounded men who were calling for help. Von Daun was compelled to say "no", for the walls were seriously damaged and a surprise attack was always a possibility.

About midnight on 29th August a French unit, led by deserters, slipped

The coat of arms of the Duc de la Feuillade, commander of the French forces at the time of the siege of Turin.

into the moats and up a flight of steps into the tunnel known as the "capitale bassa" (low capital). This led to the fortress by a passage only 200 yards long.

Pietro Micca

Piedmontese grenadiers were guarding the steps which were mined underneath. Two of the guards were experts with mines. One of these was Pietro Micca, known as "Passepartout". As soon as the grenadiers saw the French soldiers'

approach they bolted the door of the stairway. While the French were attempting to break down the door the grenadiers hastily withdrew leaving Pietro Micca and his companion to set off the mine.

The fuse for the mine was a length of cloth about three yards long which the soldiers called the "sausage". It burned very slowly to give the mine-layers time to reach safety. The longer the fuse, the longer the explosion was delayed.

Pietro and his companion realized that the door was about to give way. Pietro also realized that if he lit the fuse according to the rules the French would have the door broken down before the mine exploded, in which case they would be able to extinguish the fuse and walk into Turin.

That was when Pietro Micca made his decision. He ordered his companion to save himself and follow the grenadiers, shouting to him when he hesitated, "You take longer to go than a day without bread!" and he pushed the man out of the way. Then he shortened the fuse so that the mine would explode at the moment the French soldiers broke down the door.

He lit the fuse and threw himself down the steps. The mine exploded as Pietro was entering the tunnel and the explosion hurled him along the passageway for forty feet. His companion could hear his last cries. The name of Pietro Micca is still venerated in Italy.

Eugene arrives

Next day at dusk, while the struggle was still raging, Victor Amadeus signalled that Eugene had arrived. The defenders saw his signal fires on the Superga Hill and knew that the city would soon be freed.

Once again the French commanders were having differences of opinion. The Duke of Orleans wanted to raise the siege altogether and drew up his army for battle. His generals maintained that

it would be better to sit where they were and wait for the attack behind their defences. Louis XIV himself was brought into the argument and agreed with the generals.

So it happened that, on 7th September when the Austrian-Piedmontese army attacked, the French found themselves spread out on a long front. Their right wing, commanded by the Duke of Orleans, was annihilated by a charge of hussars and the survivors had to retreat in disorder. The left wing, stationed by the Castle of Lucente, put up a stubborn resistance before finally withdrawing.

On the retreat the troops destroyed magazines and bridges. At this point twelve battalions came out of the city and attacked the French on the flank and from the rear. Then followed hand-to-hand fighting during which Eugene was unsaddled. There was one more favourable opportunity for the French but Victor Amadeus let loose his cavalry and the situation was restored.

At 3 o'clock on 7th September, 1706, the cousins entered Turin.

Victor Amadeus in action in the last hours of the battle which ended in the relief of Turin.

This symbolic print, "The War in the East", shows a Turkish standard-bearer beside a French and British soldier, all facing the Russians.

CHAPTER 9

SEBASTOPOL

The Crimea is a large peninsula projecting from southern Russia between the Black Sea and the Sea of Azov. After a long and varied history it was conquered by the Turks in 1475. It became independent in 1774 when Catherine the Great of Russia compelled the Turks to agree to this. In 1783 it was annexed by Russia.

The Crimean War of 1853 to 1856, in which Russia was faced by an alliance of Turkey, Britain, France and the Kingdom of Sardinia-Piedmont, was a major episode in a long unsettled history. The war was really the result of Turkish suspicions of Russian expansionist designs in the Balkans. Turkey at that time was still a great empire in terms of territory, but was politically weak and decadent and generally referred to as "the sick man of Europe".

The immediate cause of the conflict was Czar Nicholas I's insistence on bringing under his protection Christians resident in the Turkish empire, while the Turks considered that their own guarantees to Christians living there should be sufficient. There were 12 million orthodox Christians in the parts of Turkey most directly threatened by Russian expansionist policy, and this was one reason why the sultan rejected the czar's overtures.

Test of strength

The Russian Orthodox Church, like the Catholic Church, already had many privileges in the holy places of the Turkish empire—the churches of the Holy Sepulchre and of the Virgin in Jerusalem, the church of the Nativity in Bethlehem and the holy place of Golgotha. Czar Nicholas felt that he could obtain Britain's support for his claims and that France need not be consulted. He decided to make the holy places a test of strength, and sent Prince Menshikov to Turkey to assert Russian rights under past treaties. But the czar was wrong in assuming that he could do

A Turkish coat of arms in the 19th century.

this without creating great concern in Great Britain.

The gathering storm

When the Russian demands were presented, the British ambassador to Turkey advised the Turks to be cautious. The Turkish Government, however, resisted them and Menshikov had to withdraw his mission. The British Government now felt that the Russian moves were designed to create a pro-

tectorate over Turkey and on 2nd June, the British fleet was ordered to set sail for the Dardanelles where it was joined the following day by French squadrons.

The Russians mobilized their Black Sea fleet to intimidate Turkey, and British suspicions increased. The appointment of Viscount Stratford de Redcliffe as British ambassador to Turkey reassured the Turks because he was well known for his anti-Russian views.

The Turks, however, rejected his overtures. Czar Nicholas then sent troops into Moldavia and Walachia, and into that part of Armenia then ruled by the Turkish empire. Part of Moldavia is today in Russia, the remainder and Walachia are in present-day Rumania.

On 4th October, 1853, the sultan issued an ultimatum announcing that fighting would break out in two weeks' time if Russian troops were not withdrawn by then. The czar did not withdraw his troops and war between Turkey and Russia broke out on 23rd October. The first fighting on land went in the Turks' favour but on 30th November Russia won a naval victory at Sinop on the Black Sea. The Crimean War had begun.

The Great Powers were alarmed by this disturbance of European equilibrium. All their efforts at pacification had failed. The "Vienna Note", issued by Britain, France, Austria and Prussia, urging the sultan to remain faithful to the letter and spirit of the Treaties of Kainardji and Adrianople relative to the protection of the Christian religion, was not acceptable to the Russians who looked upon it as a mere restatement of their proper rights. They wanted more. The Turkish attitude, that she herself would guarantee the rights of Christians in her empire, meant that all foreigners would be kept out of Turkey, whereas Russia was claiming the right of intervention.

Britain and France intervene

With the Turkish declaration of war on Russia the Great Powers intervened; but only Britain and France sent troops in the first instance, in March 1854. These were followed shortly afterwards by troops from Piedmont. At that time the head of the Sardinia-Piedmont Government, the Count of Cavour, was envisaging a united Italy under one king, Victor Emmanuel II, in place of the many small monarchies ruling a divided Italy with Austrian support. He wanted the whole world to know about it and realized that if Piedmont could have a place at the peace conference after the Crimean War, along with France and Britain, his cause could be heard.

France and Britain had invited Piedmont's intervention, but they wanted the Sardinian forces as mercenaries. Count Cavour, whose ambitions for Italy came foremost, refused this absolutely, and at the Turin Convention of 26th January, 1855, an agreement was reached. Article 6 of this read: "Their Majesties the Emperor of the French and the Queen of the United Kingdom of Great Britain and Ireland will guarantee the integrity of the States of His Majesty the King of Sardinia and undertake to defend them against any attack for the duration of this present war".

It was feared that eventually Austria might take advantage of the situation to attack Piedmont, but Austria made no move.

Gallipoli landings

On 31st March, 1854, the first French contingents disembarked at Gallipoli in the Dardanelles under the command of General François Certain Canrobert. In May another 50,000 French troops under the command of Marshal Jacques Leroy de Saint-Arnaud and 25,000 British troops under the command of

This contemporary print shows a French drum major taking a pinch of snuff.

Fitzroy James Henry Somerset, Lord Raglan, set foot on Turkish territory.

The decision to attack Russia in the Crimea was largely dictated by the fact that Sebastopol, which had already been made into a Russian naval base by Catherine II, had become an arsenal so well stocked as to guarantee complete military control over the whole of the Black Sea. Sebastopol was, therefore, a symbol of Russian aggressiveness and power and attracted the allies as such bastions had done before and were to do again.

The generals

The siege was not decided on immediately. Before the set-piece battle was even planned there was a series of actions between allied and Russian forces which are now considered by historians to be the worst examples of the art of war in modern times.

Lord Raglan, who was sixty-six years of age and in command of the British Expeditionary Force, had learned nothing since the battle of Waterloo in 1815, when he was on Wellington's staff. The other British commanders were nearly as old and had as little or even less experience than he. The French commander, Saint-Arnaud, died soon after the landings and the French command was taken over by Canrobert who was a good soldier but whose relations with Lord Raglan could not have been worse. In May 1855 Canrobert was replaced by General Aimable Pélissier.

From Varna, which is now part of Bulgaria, the allied troops were sent to their assembly point, thirty-one miles north of Sebastopol, in ships that were too small for their numbers. Never had so many soldiers been transported by sea in a single campaign. There was chaos instead of organization, provisions were scarce, equipment poor and sanitary arrangements almost non-existent. Cholera raged uncontrolled among the soldiers.

March on Sebastopol

Between 14th and 16th September, the French and British troops disembarked on the Crimea and on the 19th the march on Sebastopol began. Before they could reach it, however, they had to cross the River Alma, along whose banks were drawn up 33,000 Russian soldiers under the command of Prince Alexander Menshikov, Governor of Finland and Minister of the Imperial Navy.

Prince Menshikov had been the czar's ambassador-extraordinary to Constantinople during the negotiations with the Turks over the holy places. The sultan's rejection of his proposals had been a blow to him. Now he had something else to be embittered about, for he was defeated on the banks of the Alma and had to flee from there after five hours' fighting, leaving large numbers of his men as prisoners or casualties. Luckily for the survivors of his army, the allied commanders had no idea how to organize a pursuit, otherwise the Crimean War might have ended on that same day, 20th September 1854.

But Marshal Saint-Arnaud was ill with cholera and unable to give directions. Lord Raglan was also unable to give directions because he had no idea how to give them. While the French commander was embarking for France (he was to die at sea on 29th September) Canrobert and Raglan made the decision to besiege Sebastopol.

To the north the city was undefended but, incomprehensibly, the allies decided to attack it from the south. This meant a long and difficult march all round the city through an area without water. At last the soldiers came in sight of the Russian Côte d'Azur, the southern border of the Crimea, dotted with pleasant villages.

Balaklava

The British set up their general headquarters in one of these villages, Bala-

klava. During its defence the British fought an action that has become known to history as the Charge of the Light Brigade—one of the most senseless massacres in all history. Six hundred British cavalrymen, using sabres and lances, attacked the Russian artillery with incredible gallantry and élan, and were cut to pieces.

Meanwhile the Russians had withdrawn into the Sebastopol defences. To protect the city from the sea they blocked the entrance to the port by sinking ships there. On 5th November the opposing forces clashed at Inkerman, a village at the mouth of the Chernaya River. Here the Russians attacked the British camp in force, with no other result than the loss of 20,000 men. The British army fought what has come to be known as "a soldier's battle", without direction or leadership, but were victorious.

Other actions were fought round the city and these were largely the result of the incompetence of commanders. They failed to cut communications between the city and the hinterland and so allowed reinforcements and supplies to arrive regularly. At one stage the siege was reduced to an artillery battle. Both sides had brought ashore the heaviest cannon from their ships and these were manned by sailors acting as gunners.

Stalemate

The weeks dragged on and despite the relative mildness of the local climate the coming of winter brought operations to a standstill. The two armies drawn up on the opposite banks of the Chernaya River contented themselves with an occasional gun duel.

Cavour meanwhile had achieved his

An everyday scene in the field in the Crimea. French soldiers in their camp during a pause in the fighting.

aims by diplomacy and now 15,000 Piedmontese soldiers set sail from Genoa under the command of General Alfonso La Marmora, whose second division was commanded by his brother Alexander, the creator of the crack Italian infantry regiment the Bersaglieri.

The Sardinian army arrived in the Crimea on 8th May, 1855. On the 19th, Canrobert had a disagreement with Lord Raglan and left the Crimea. Command of the French Expeditionary Force now passed to Aimable Pélissier, remembered for his massacre of 600 Arab men, women and children in Algeria in 1830.

On 18th June, 1855, it was at last decided to make a first assault on Sebastopol. This failed. Ten days later Lord Raglan died of cholera and his command passed to General James Simpson. On 16th August the Piedmontese infantry were engaged for the first time at the battle of Cernaia.

Russians besieged

The besieged Russians were given plenty of time to improve their defences while the British army was held back waiting for a preliminary bombardment by their own artillery. Russian men, women and children worked at the defences day and night under the direction of Colonel Todleben.

While the siege guns were being dragged into position there was ample evidence that the Russians would defend Sebastopol stoutly. The great question is why the Russians were ever allowed to augment their defences without interruption. The British soldiers were to pay for this later when the attacks developed.

The bombardment by seventy-three British and fifty-three French guns began at dawn on 17th October by which date the army had been marking time within sight of the Russian defences for three weeks.

Everybody expected Sebastopol to be blasted from its foundations within two days, but it did not turn out that way.

Russian artillery strikes

The forty-eight hour bombardment did not materialize. The Russian artillery, traditionally accurate and well-served, fulfilled its rôle here to upset the besiegers' plans. They put the French artillery out of action for two days and blew up a magazine.

Each night the defenders managed to service their guns and keep them in action after damage from the British artillery. The bombardment of the fortress by the fleet in the bay contributed little to the assault. After a week Sebastopol's defences were still intact and it was obvious that the artillery attack was not going to destroy

An early episode in the Crimean War – the savage and bloody battle of the River Alma on 20th September, 1854. In the foreground the British guards are advancing under the command of the Duke of Cambridge. The illustration is a contemporary Austrian print.

them despite the fact that everything was being concentrated on the siege.

Assault by infantry

According to the words of an official report prepared by General Pélissier, "the attacking infantry on the right wing opened up a more intense fire against the Malakoff fort and the defences nearest to the enemy, in order to allow the engineers' corps to prepare the closest possible area to the place, to dig the trenches from which the troops could make a rush on the fortifications. The engineers, furthermore, prepared the attacking and scaling machines. On 5th September our batteries on the left opened fire most violently on the city. As everything was ready I resolved, in agreement with General Simpson, to fix the hour of the attack at midday on 8th September."

And that was what happened. At exactly 12 o'clock on the 8th September, the French General MacMahon's Zouaves made an irrepressible dash onto the parapets of the Malakoff fort which was the key to the whole defence.

The British infantry attacked another strong point, the so called "Great Redan". Despite a very rough sea the allied fleets joined in the action from the bay, bombarding in their turn

another section of the fortifications. Here and there Russian counter-attacks forced the allied infantry back into the trenches but the whole of the defensive ring was now engaged and Pélissier could concentrate his efforts on the Malakoff fort.

MacMahon persists

MacMahon persisted in his determination to take the fort even when a powder magazine blew up on his left with a terrifying explosion and three Russian columns risked everything in an attempt to recapture the fort. MacMahon's words are now historic "J'y suis, j'y reste" (Here I am and here I stay).

"By now", Pélissier's report goes on, "Malakoff was in our hands and no one could recapture it. It was half past four in the afternoon. Immediately all arrangements had been made for coping with an eventual enemy counter-attack by night. But our uncertainty did not last long. Darkness had hardly fallen when fires were lit everywhere. Mines exploded, powder magazines were blown into the air and the sight of Sebastopol in flames, burnt down by the Russians themselves, appeared to the eyes of the whole army as one of the most impressive and one of the

saddest sights in all the history of war."

Tolstoy's account

Tolstoy describes the scene inside the fortress. "Along the whole line of the ramparts of Sebastopol, where for so many months a remarkably dynamic life had been going on, which had for so many months seen dying heroes give in to death, one after another, and which for so many months had excited the fear, the hatred and finally the admiration of the enemy—on the ramparts of Sebastopol there was no longer a single person.

Everything was dead, deserted frightening, but not quiet. Everything was still falling into ruin. On the ground, still trembling and broken up by the recent explosions, lay smashed gun-carriages on top of corpses, pits, splinters of beams and of armour, and more bodies—silent, in grey and blue overcoats. All these were still frequently shaken and lit up by the crimson glow of the explosions, which continued to rend the air."

Russian retreat

Using a bridge of boats strung across the bay, the Russians were able to retreat under cover of darkness. The mines, which went on exploding in their rear prevented any pursuit by the allies and the bridge was destroyed when the last of the Russian soldiers had made the crossing.

Leo Tolstoy was among the troops retreating from Sebastopol. He was then twenty-six years of age, and was later to write *War and Peace* and become a literary figure of world stature.

In his *Tales of Sebastopol*, he left a vivid description of the retreat:— "The enemies saw that something incomprehensible was going on in that menacing Sebastopol. Those explosions and that deathly silence on the battlements made them tremble; but they dared not believe, still being under the influence of that day's strong and calm resistance, that the uncrushable adversary had disappeared, and motionless, in silence, they anxiously awaited the end of that dismal night.

The army in Sebastopol, like the sea on a black and stormy night, joined up, separated and anxiously quivered in its entire mass; it moved towards the bay in a wave, to the bridge and to Sievernaia; it moved slowly through the impenetrable darkness, away from the place where were left so many courageous brothers, from the place which was steeped in their blood, from the place which they had for eleven

A Cossack lance from the Artillery Museum in Turin.

months defended against an enemy twice their strength."

Terrible casualties

British and French forces suffered terrible casualties in their assaults on the Sebastopol fortress. The British attack on the Redan in September failed with heavy losses, despite the great gallantry of the troops involved.

The ordinary soldiers who had rescued the reputations of their generals at Alma and the Inkerman could not do so at Sebastopol, the story of their failure being written in their own blood. For the British army, Sebastopol was another soldiers' battle. It has been said that at one period every second bed in the hospitals contained a dead man.

Tales of Sebastopol

Inside the fortress casualties were also mounting and Tolstoy describes one bombardment; "Suddenly a frightful roar, which shakes not only your organs of hearing, but your whole being, startles you so that you begin to shake all over. Then you hear the whistle of the shot as it goes away, and a thick cloud of dust covers you, the platform and the black figures of the sailors moving about above. 'It has fallen right in the gunport; seems to have killed two . . . they've been taken away . . .' you hear someone exclaiming joyfully. 'There, now they're angry; they'll fire here now,' someone will say; and in fact, a moment later, you see a flash, smoke; the sentry standing on the parapet shouts 'Can-non!' And immediately afterwards a ball whistles past you hits the ground and scatters a shower of dirt and stones around it. You are startled to hear a man groaning. You go up to the wounded man, at the same time as the stretcher; in the blood and mud he has a strange inhuman look."

Only Tolstoy could have written

such a graphic account. On every page there emerge unforgettable pictures of the soldiers who took part in that bloody epic, their sacrifices, their mistakes, their fears, and their heroism. But a message that comes clearly, despite the author's deep sympathy and total involvement, is an absolute condemnation of the horrors of war and its futility. No one seeking an insight into this tragic campaign could do better than read Tolstoy.

The young Tolstoy had a firm belief in final victory. He was youthful and patriotic and this comes out in one of his stories which describes the situation on the fourth rampart in Sebastopol. It is said that the Czarina Alexandra wept when she read the concluding lines of the first part of the three *Tales of Sebastopol*.

Russell and Florence Nightingale

The sufferings of the soldiers in the Crimean War have often been described but are really beyond description. The number of dead in the campaign on all sides has been put as high as 250,000 Little was known of the privations of soldiers in action, or the deaths from starvation and disease, or how the

wounded were neglected and allowed to die in the vilest conditions until a journalist—William Howard Russell of *The Times*—sent home his reports. For the first time people at home became aware of the real horrors of the Crimea.

The Crimea had many heroes whose names will never be known, but one name stands out above all others – Florence Nightingale, an English woman born in Florence in 1820.

When war broke out in the Crimea, she was superintendent of a London hospital for women. Authorized by the British government to organize sanitary arrangements for the wounded and the sick in the Crimea, Florence Nightingale set up centres at the British base of Scutari in Turkey and elsewhere. Her example and methods of organization were responsible for the founding some years later of the International Red Cross by the Swiss philanthropist, Jean Henri Dunant.

Florence Nightingale is now remembered as the "lady of the lamp" because of the romantic conception of her as the ministering angel carrying light into darkness. She certainly carried cleanliness and compassion into the midst of suffering and became the symbol of the Red Cross nurse.

Two photographs taken on the field at Sebastopol at the end of the siege. On the left, the ruined city, above the tower of Malakoff.

French hussars, under the command of General d'Allonville, charging the Russian infantry in one of the final assaults.

CHAPTER 10

LENINGRAD AND STALINGRAD

One of the great sieges of the Second World War was that of Leningrad which was totally surrounded by the Germans from the summer of 1941 until March 1943.

Leningrad was highly vulnerable to a major assault and it was Russian awareness of this that made them go to war with Finland in 1939 to gain space for manoeuvre round Leningrad. The Finnish campaign ended after the breach of their Mannerheim Line on the Karelian Isthmus and Stalin was able to extend his frontier to cushion any assault on Leningrad. In the event, the Germans still reached Leningrad and were able to invest it but not to take it.

A scrap of paper

Hitler had long planned to attack the U.S.S.R. but he was not ready in 1939. He had decided to crush France first. Accordingly he signed a pact with Stalin in order to gain time. This pact became known to history as the Nazi-Soviet pact, but Hitler's intention was to break it as soon as it suited him.

The German invasion begins

The code name for the German attack on Russia was Barbarossa, meaning Red Beard, nickname of the great German hero, King Frederick I. Up to the time of the German attack, Stalin had meticulously fulfilled all his agreements with Nazi Germany and was reluctant to believe reports of an impending attack, disregarding all warnings including a direct warning from Winston Churchill.

The result was that when Hitler launched the Wehrmacht and the Luftwaffe against Russia on 22nd June, 1941, the Red Army was caught almost wholly unprepared, and entire units were annihilated or taken prisoner in the greatest frontier battle in all history.

The Wehrmacht attacked in three army groups. Army group north drove on Leningrad. Commanded by General von Leeb it was formed of the Sixteenth and Eighteenth Armies and the Hoepner Armoured Group and organized in twenty-six divisions. These made a rapid advance, sweeping the Red Army from their path. The Soviet Army of the Baltic was cut off and the Wehrmacht's army group north set its sights on Leningrad. Von Leeb split his forces into three columns when he was ninety-three miles from the city and they converged on it from three directions, gripping it as in a vice.

Leningrad isolated

The encirclement was not immediately completed. During five days of bitter fighting the Red Army held out in the old Czarist fortress of Schlüsselburg and kept open a narrow corridor to the east. This was their only line of communication with the hinterland and Moscow, and their only supply route.

Autumn 1942. The Germans advance through the ruins of Stalingrad. At this time they were still sure of conquering the city.

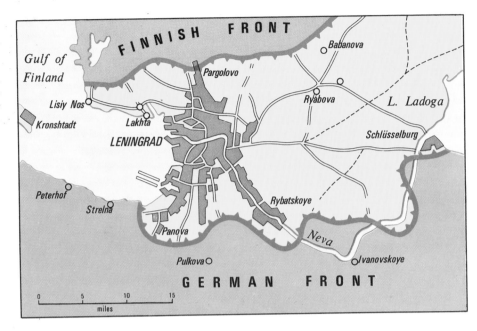

Plan of the encirclement of Leningrad. The city is held by the pincers of the Finnish and German armies. The city was never occupied but was almost destroyed by continuous bombing and shelling.

But at the end of the five days the Germans had taken Schlüsselburg and Leningrad was totally isolated, its last overland link cut with the rest of the country.

All that remained were the waterways, the Gulf of Finland on the west and Lake Ladoga in the north-east. These remained open and supplies trickled to the besieged garrison and to the people despite all attempts by the German and Finnish fleets and aircraft to cut them off. The Finns had allied themselves with the Germans in their attack on Russia, a contingency that Stalin had always taken into account.

The people resist

Retreating armies and refugees fleeing before the Germans all fell back on Leningrad and the population suddenly swelled to five million. The city organized itself for defence.

Every man, woman and child played some part in constructing defence systems—anti-tank traps and outer rings of trenches. Buildings were blown up one by one and transformed into fortresses.

The half-completed stadium was dismantled and redoubts and artillery emplacements were created out of the material thus collected. The people of Leningrad, like the soldiers, were determined that their city would never fall to the Germans.

The factories continued in full operation, despite German air raids and shelling, turning out ammunition, weapons and even tanks. The Kirov factory, known in the Czarist era as Putilov, formed its workers into a special unit known as the Civil Guard of Leningrad. The Kirov factory was named after the leader of the Leningrad Bolsheviks. The Kirov Civil Guard acted as an assault force, engaging the German soldiers in the kind of fighting they least liked—hand-to-hand combat. Other workers' units were formed within the city to defend and counter-attack.

Railway on ice

The supplies within the city were organized. Strict rationing was introduced. Substitute foods were developed, fuel was conserved. But eventually the population was reduced almost to starvation level and thousands of people perished of hunger in the streets.

In the winter of 1942, the Leningraders succeeded in establishing a link with the outside world by building a railway across the frozen surface of Lake Ladoga. This was kept open as long as the ice was able to carry traffic, but the supplies were meagre in relation to the city's needs and people continued to die.

The winter of 1942 was severe and every effort was made to provide heat. Leningrad had been a coaling port for half a century. The city's organization decided to dredge the Neva and from it 5,000 tons of coal were recovered. In the fight against hunger the inhabitants used every unit of cultivable ground for the growing of vegetables, especially cabbages.

Return of the Red Army

In December 1942, the Red Army recaptured the Schlüsselburg fortress. This dramatic coup improved not only morale, which was never really low, but eased the general situation.

The Germans went on butting until 18th January, 1943, when they withdrew from the assault. The city, however, remained almost entirely cut off until finally relieved by the Red Army on 27th January, 1944. On that day the Russians announced the relief of Leningrad.

A German soldier with the equipment he carried during the Russian campaign.
The weapons are —
1, The MP-40, a 32 shot automatic pistol.
2, The Walther P-38, an 8 round, 9 mm. pistol.
3, KAR-98K, 5 shot, 7·9 mm. rifle.
4, A hand grenade.

Approach to Stalingrad

Although the siege of Leningrad lasted for 900 days, it was the great siege-like battle of Stalingrad that captured the imagination of the world and brought universal praise to the Red Army.

Germans halted

Stalingrad was named after Joseph Vissarionovich Stalin who had defended the city during the War of Intervention following the Revolution of 1917. Before that it had been called Tsaritsyn.

The very name of the city was a great attraction to Hitler and he decided to aim a mortal blow at it. At first, the Wehrmacht's rampaging Panzer divisions appeared irresistible and the world looked for the collapse of Russia in a matter of weeks or months.

But the Russian winter came and slowed down the attack and the Red Army was given time to reorganize and to move vital industries out of the zone of the armies. The assault against Stalingrad was launched in August, 1942 and Paulus's Sixth army was in sight of the city on 6th September.

To take the city was their objective. Its capture would mean control of its great industries and of a navigable river, the Volga, which was the most important waterway in the entire Soviet Union. To control Stalingrad was essential to the plan of the three army groups—north against Moscow, the centre against Stalingrad and the south towards the petroleum fields of the Caucasus.

A typical piece of Russian armament, the 120 mm mortar, type 38. It fired 16 KG bombs a distance of over 4 miles. The complete weapon weighed over 400 pounds.

Paulus assaults

Before the assault on the city began, its population was about half a million, the majority of the inhabitants being industrial workers. The famous Dzershinsky factory was capable of turning out 10,000 tractors a year, but at the outbreak of the Second World War, it

had been transformed into a tank factory.

Equally famous were the Red October steelworks, founded in 1897, which were soon to be bitterly fought over by Russians and Germans.

The Germans, convinced they could take Stalingrad by storm and at no great cost, committed only Paulus's Sixth Army and the Third Rumanian Division supported by the Eighth Air Corps under the command of von Richthofen. They surrounded the city on the landward side but left the Volga crossings open from the east bank.

This was the only way in which the Red Army could ferry across reinforcements. The optimism of the Germans stemmed from their quite mistaken belief that the Russian army no longer existed.

Russia gathers strength

In fact, on the south side of the Volga, fresh, well-trained divisions were massing, troops equipped with the most sophisticated weapons—T34 tanks, the great multiple rocket launcher Katuska and self-propelled guns. At the same time other Russian forces were assembling at Voronezh in the north to launch an encircling attack on the German Sixth Army.

The Germans could not have foreseen any of this. For months their Panzer divisions and infantry had surged forward with broken, straggling units retreating before them. Divisions were broken up and left to their own devices and the German advance went on at blitzkrieg speed. They had pursued the Russians to the Don, taken possession of that river and their momentum had carried them to Stalingrad.

A German anti-aircraft gun on the Leningrad front.

German supply train on the Steppes near Stalingrad. Although the armies were highly mechanized, both sides also used horses and mules for transport.

Stalingrad crumbles

Hitler's orders were that Stalingrad had to be taken by 25th August. On the 23rd Paulus reached the Volga, north of the city in which 40,000 Russian civilians died from an attack by 600 bomber aircraft. But 300,000 managed to escape beyond the river. Those who stayed shut themselves up in air raid shelters and waited along with the soldiers of the 62nd Soviet Division.

By 23rd September, almost the entire city was in German hands. Two districts remained in the hands of the Red Army and it was in the fight for these two districts that the German force was broken.

Stalingrad spreads out along the west bank of the Volga for a distance of twenty-five miles. In the centre is the railway station. Paulus knew that if he captured the railway station he would cut the city in two and this is what he tried to do with a series of local attacks.

Each attack was followed by counter-attack and each cost the lives of thousands of men, Russian and German. The battle dragged on into October and the Germans reached the Volga on the south of the city, but the house to house fighting continued—fierce, difficult, chaotic. Every ruined house was a fortress. Tanks rumbled through the streets.

Men fought from house to house and from one heap of rubble to another, searching in every room, killing and being killed.

Wall by wall, Stalingrad crumbled while the year wore on and the first patches of ice filmed the Volga heralding the coming of winter which was what the Germans feared most.

German Sixth army trapped

Paulus could probably have taken the city if he had concentrated on the ferries carrying troops to the west bank, and it has often been said that he fought the wrong battle. On Christmas Day,

1942, he was awaiting supplies. General Hoth, nicknamed in the German army "poison dwarf", was some fifty miles from Stalingrad in command of the Fourth Army. Following his army was a column of trucks carrying thousands of tons of supplies intended for Paulus's Sixth Army.

But Paulus was now trapped, encircled. If he could have broken out and reached Hoth the Sixth Army would have been saved. But his tanks were held up for want of fuel. They could travel only eighteen miles and then they would grind to a complete halt. Thus Hoth would have to advance to meet them; but this he was unable to do and

The Russian front in October 1942. The German advance appears irresistible. Advance units are less than 65 miles from Moscow but Hitler halts them there and switches his main attack towards the south.

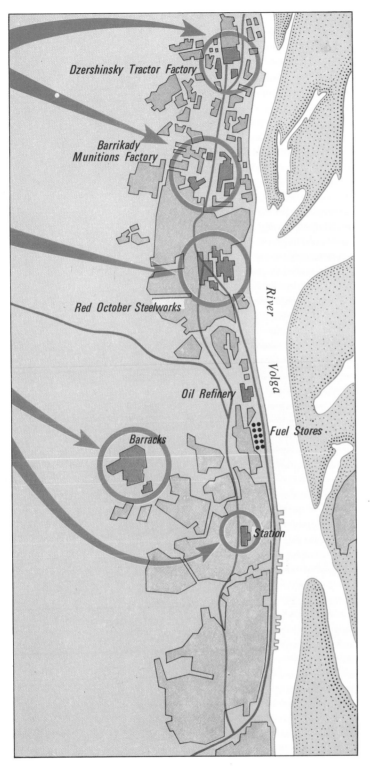

Labels on map:
Dzershinsky Tractor Factory
Barrikady Munitions Factory
Red October Steelworks
Oil Refinery
Barracks
Fuel Stores
Station
River
Volga

Stalingrad, now called Volgograd, stretches out along the right bank of the Volga. Arrows indicate key points and objectives of the attacking Germans.

he and his forces were soon committed elsewhere.

Collapse on the Don

The Italian Eighth Army had collapsed on the Don and was in full retreat before the Russians. The road to Rostov was now open to the Red Army and if they reached that city one million Germans would be trapped. Hoth, therefore, decided to take the offensive against Malinovski's Red Army, attacking it from the rear from the other side of the Volga.

It was at this point that the Fourth German Army abandoned the attempt to rescue Paulus's Sixth.

No withdrawal

In the city itself, a sniper's battle still raged. House to house fighting continued, especially in the centre of the city, but the Germans were finished. The German High Command favoured abandoning Stalingrad and strengthening the front as a whole but Hitler was adamant that the city had to be held. On 11th November, von Paulus launched his last, useless offensive.

On 19th November, the bombardment by heavy Soviet artillery threw the Rumanian line into confusion and an avalanche of tanks fell upon them. On the 22nd two Soviet armoured corps crossed the Volga north and south and met in the dawn at Paulus's rear. The German Sixth Army was encircled.

Hitler now authorized Paulus to make an attempt to break out towards the south and meet up with Hoth. But on Christmas Day 1942, Hoth fell back on Kotelnikovo, while in Stalingrad the Russians recaptured the Red October factory.

Russian offensive

On 10th January at 8.03 a.m., 6,000 Soviet guns opened fire on what was

Uniform, equipment and weapons of the Russian defenders of Stalingrad.
1. M-1930, 7.62 mm rifle. 2. PPSH, 7.62 mm automatic carbine.
3. Tokarev TT 7.62 mm pistol.
4. Hand Grenade.
Note the standard calibre of all small arms.

The remains of the "Red October" factory in Stalingrad where the fiercest fighting took place.

Stalingrad after the battle. The Germans are in full retreat. The wreckage of a Messerschmitt rears above the ruins of the city like a symbol of defeat.

left of the German Sixth Army. Twenty-five thousand Germans died on that day. On 23rd January the Russians once again offered terms of surrender to Paulus but he refused. On the 26th Russian reinforcements under Rokossovsky linked up with Zhukov's troops, who had held the eastern part of the city throughout the attack.

On 30th January, Paulus sent word to Hitler that the Sixth Army could hold out for no more than twenty-four hours and that it would resist to the last man and the last round of

ammunition for "the Führer and the Fatherland". Hitler replied by making Paulus a field marshal, then he waited for news of his suicide, for no German field marshal had ever fallen alive into the hands of an enemy.

At 19.45 hours on 31st January, 1943, the last message was transmitted, "the Russians are at the entrance to the bunker. We are destroying radio equipment." Shortly afterwards, Field Marshal Paulus was seated before Generals Rokossovsky and Voronov. He was their prisoner.

ACKNOWLEDGEMENTS

Biblioteca dell'Istituto Internazionale di Studi Liguri, Bordighera: pp. 44,76. Biblioteca Militare Centrale, Rome: pp. 50, 72 (bottom), 88. Biblioteca del Museo d'Armi Antiche della Pusterla di Sant'Ambrogio, Milan: pp. 12, 14 (right), 19, 39. Biblioteca del Museo Navale, Genoa: pp. 26 (bottom), 65. Bibliothèque du Musée de l'Armée, Paris: pp. 17, 56 (right), 61, 69, 72 (top), 87, 100 & 101, 103, 105, 107, 108 & 109, 111. Bibliothèque Nationale, Cabinet des Estampes, Paris: pp. 11, 14 (left), 16 (bottom), 92, 98. Bibliothèque Publique et Universitaire, Geneva: pp. 57, 59. Civica Raccolta delle Stampe "Achille Bertarelli", Milan: pp. 10 (top), 12 & 13, 18 (top), 23, 28 & 29, 30, 36 & 37, 40 (top), 47, 55, 58 64, 73, 74 (top), 75 (top), 86, 102. De Laurentiis, R.A.I.: p. 33. Gabinetto Fotografico Nazionale del Ministero della Pubblica Istruzione, Rome: p. 36. Galleria Civica dd'Arte Moderna, Turin: pp. 76 & 77. Istituto e Museo dell'Arma del Genio, Rome: p. 96. Vezio Melegari: pp. 63, 99. Municipio di Crema: p. 15. Musée des Beaux-Arts, Dijon: p. 6. Musée des Beaux-Arts, Gand: pp. 52 & 53. Musée des Beaux-Arts de la Ville de Paris, Paris: endpaper. Musée de la Tour de l'Orle d'Or, Sémur: pp. 44 & 45. Musée Massena, Nice: pp. 70, 74 (bottom), 78, 79. Museo della Civilta Romana, Rome: pp. 38, 40 (bottom), 43. Museo Nazionale del Risorgimento, Turin: p. 90. Museo Pietro Micca, Turin: pp. 91, 94, 95, 97. Museo del Risorgimento Nazionale, Milan: p. 106. Museo di Roma, Rome: pp. 22, 31. Museo della Scienza e della Tecnica, Milan: p. 16 (top). Museo Storico Nazionale d'Artiglieria, Turin: p. 109 (bottom). Palacio del Senado, Madrid: p. 62. Pinacoteca Vaticana: p. 82. Rizzoli: pp. 10 (bottom), 89. 112, 116 & 117, 118 & 119, 121 (bottom). "Soldatino": pp. 8, 10 (top), 15, 34, 42, 66, 75 (bottom and right), 80, 81. Studio dell'Illustrazione Frederico Arborio Mella: pp. 48, 53, 54, 56 (left), 92 & 93. Vojenske Muzeum, Prague: pp. 84 & 85.

Photographs by Bosi: pp. 24, 29 (bottom), 60, 67, 68 & 69. Bulloz: endpaper. Camera Press: pp. 122 & 123. Cassin: pp. 25, 32. Dani: pp. 6, 8, 10 (top), 12, 12 & 13, 14 (right), 15, 17, 18 (top), 19 22, 23, 26 (bottom), 28 & 29, 30, 31, 34, 37, 38 (bottom), 39, 40 (top), 42, 44, 44 & 45, 47, 50 55, 56 (right), 58, 61, 64, 65, 66, 69, 72, 73, 74, 75, 76, 76 & 77, 78, 79, 80, 81, 82, 87, 88, 91, 96, 100 & 101, 102, 103, 105, 106, 107, 108 & 109, 109, 110 & 111, 111. Dulevant: p. 90. Giraudon: pp. 52 & 53, 84 & 85. Lunel: p. 16 (top). Mairani: pp. 48, 53, 54, 56 (left). Mandel: p. 51. M.A.S., Barcelona: p. 62. Publications Filmées d'Art et d'Histoire, Mautrange: p. 16 (bottom). Scala: pp. 26 (top), 27. Scalfati: pp. 57, 59. Service Photographique du Cabinet des Estampes de la Bibliothèque Nationale, Paris: pp. 11, 14 (left), 92, 98.

Designs and Drawings by Deirdre Amsden: pp. 115, 121. John Batchelor: pp. 20 & 21, 116. Etrusco: pp. 18 & 19, 30, 41, 42, 73, 114, 119, 120.

Cover "Soldatino", photographed by Dani.

BIBLIOGRAPHY

Brown, R. A., *Castles.* Batsford (London), 1954.

Fitzgerald, E., *The British Army.* Oxford University Press, 1964.

Green, R. L., *The Tale of Troy.* Puffin Book (London), 1967.

Hayward, J. F., *European Armour.* H.M.S.O. 1965.

Pruller, W., *Diary of a German Soldier.* Faber (London), 1963.

Sellman, R. R., *The Crusdaes.* Methuen (London), 1961.

Sheppard, E. W., *War.* Studio Vista (London), 1967.

Sorrell, A., *Living History.* Batsford (London), 1965.

Stoye, J., *The Siege of Vienna.* Collins (London), 1964.

Sutcliffe, R., *The Eagle of the Ninth.* Oxford University Press, 1954.

The Crimean War. Jackdaw No.11. Cape (London)

Watson, J. W., *The Iliad and the Odyssey.* Hamlyn (London), 1967.

Werth, A., *Russia at War.* Pan Books (London), 1965.

Woodham Smith, Cecil, *The Reason Why.* Penguin, 1957.